D1361359

Too Young to Fight

Memories from Our Youth During World War II

Compiled by Priscilla Galloway

TOO YOUNG

MEMORIES FROM OUR YOUTH DURING WORLD WAR II

TO FIGHT

Book design by Blair Kerrigan/Glyphics

Published in Canada in 1999 by
Stoddart Kids
a division of Stoddart Publishing Co. Limited
34 Lesmill Road
Toronto, ON M3B 2T6
Tel (416) 445-3333 Fax (416) 445-5967
email: Customer.Service@ccmailgw.genpub.com

Published in the United States in 2000 by
Stoddart Kids,
a division of Stoddart Publishing Co. Limited
180 Varick Street, 9th Floor
New York, New York 10014
Toll free 1-800-805-1083
email: gdsinc@genpub.com

Distributed in Canada by
General Distribution Services
325 Humber College Blvd.
Toronto, ON M9W 7C3
Tel (416) 213-1919 Fax (416) 213-1917
email: Customer.Service@ccmailgw.genpub.com

Distributed in the United States by
General Distribution Services
85 River Rock Drive, Suite 202
Buffalo, New York 14207
Toll free 1-800-805-1083
email: gdsinc@genpub.com

Canadian Cataloguing in Publication Data

Main entry under title:

Too young to fight: memories from our youth during WWII

Includes index.
ISBN 0-7737-3190-3

1. World War, 1939-1945 – Children – Biography. 2. World War, 1939-1945 – Personal narratives, Canadian. 3. Authors, Canadian (English) – 20th century – Biography.* I. Galloway, Priscilla, 1930- .

D810.C4T66 1999 940.53'161'092271 C99-930796-7

We acknowledge for their financial support of our publishing program the Canada Council, the Ontario Arts Council, and the Government of Canada through the Book Publishing Industry Development Program (BPIDP).

Printed and bound in Canada

To the student who asked if
World War II made any difference in my life,
and to the families (mine and ten others)
who produced the authors of this book.

Priscilla Galloway

Acknowledgements

I acknowledge with thanks the following contributions:

The Canadian Children's Book Centre, for including me on the 1996 Cross-Canada Book Week tour, in the course of which, a student asked an important question.

Staff and students I visited at Johnsview Village P.S., York Region District School Board, Ontario.

Syd Charendoff for generous access to his amazing World War II collection.

My writing group, for twelve years of mutual support.

Copyright Acknowledgements

INTRODUCTION

World War II began in September, 1939. Now, sixty years later, the publication of *Too Young to Fight* honours the memories of those times.

The book had its genesis during an author visit in November 1996, as I lunched and chatted with my host school's student council. Dessert was almost finished, and my mind moving toward my afternoon sessions, when a grade 8 student observed, "We looked up when you were born. You were our age when World War II was going on. Did the war make any difference in your life?"

It was not a casual question, but not a high priority one either. The students' own knowledge and experience led them to assume that World War II had made little or no difference to me. No guns were fired in Canada, after all; no bombs were dropped. The questioner's family had emigrated from India, not far from the border of Pakistan. Others at the table had come from the Near East; their own ears had heard sounds of guns and bombs. All readily acknowledged that life would change drastically for children who lived in countries torn by war; they knew that many such children had suffered and died. However, these bright young people knew nothing about the impact of World War II on civilians in Canada. They were fascinated and eager to learn more.

I went away knowing there would be a book, but with no sense of what that book might be. Now, three years later, *Too Young to Fight* provides eleven different replies to the student's question, from a galaxy of star Canadian authors. This book is about ordinary families and changes brought about by war in countries that never suffered an enemy invasion. Those changes were varied and far-reaching, more so than many readers might suspect.

The authors' collective experiences span this country from Victoria to Halifax and extend beyond Canada to the USA and UK. Two stories begin in the Far East. The youngest contributor was two years old when the war began; the oldest was twenty when it ended. Everyone's life changed, although the author's age at the time affects the story. A young child's experiences are bound to be different from those of a teenager. At the beginning of her tale, Jean Little hid under her seat in a movie theatre. By the end of hers, Monica Hughes was (finally) old enough to enlist.

Although the war caused huge changes in our lives, younger children in this sample showed less awareness of those changes than older ones. In the fashion of the time, we young people were not consulted about family plans; our feelings did not play a part in our parents' decisions. In fairness to our parents, often they themselves must have felt powerless.

Every family's experience was unique; however, interesting common threads weave through the various chapters. Six fathers were wounded in health and spirits, although only one served overseas. Four of the young authors were separated from their fathers for years. Six families were uprooted and moved, including one that was interned. None of these families got rich; many became impoverished. The war years were the crucible in which our writing selves were formed.

The authors are Priscilla Galloway (editor and contributor), Roch Carrier, Christopher Chapman, Brian Doyle, Dorothy Joan Harris, Monica Hughes, Joy Kogawa and Timothy Nakayama, Jean Little, Janet Lunn, Claire Mackay and Budge Wilson. It was difficult to decide on an appropriate order for the chapters; eventually the editors arranged them according to the first date mentioned in each one.

This book has been a labour of love, but a Herculean labour nonetheless. Usually, an editor selects existing material for an anthology. If one piece does not work, another can be found. This project, however, was full of unknowns. Every author I approached recognized the importance of the book and liked the idea of being part of it. Many made a commitment in principle immediately, although I could give them no details about publication or payment. I was moved by their confidence and delighted by their enthusiasm.

I knew they were outstanding professionals, but every writer knows that the road from concept to finished product is full of unpredictable potholes. Many authors were involved. None of us is young. What were the probabilities that some catastrophe would prevent at least one of the group from completing the work in a way that satisfied our own high standards? However, bad luck did not happen. Hard work did. And lo, the book, as planned, exists!

Black and white photos from family albums or from archival sources enrich the text. Ten authors managed to contribute at least one photograph. Sometimes it was the only surviving image they possessed. As Monica Hughes pointed out, "Film was hard to get in those years. We did not have a camera. Nobody took photos the way they do today." Some authors found ways to augment the visual element in their story; a few had many photos to choose from. It is an eclectic collection, an appropriate visual counterpoint to the stories.

Marketing the book was like selling a house from a set of plans. This proposed house, however, had one architect but a different designer for every room. The knowledge, skills and hard work of my agents, David and Lynn Bennett of Transatlantic Literary Agency, were essential, and went far beyond any agent's usual involvement.

Kathryn Cole of Stoddart Kids has been an ideal in-house editor and facilitator. She fell in love with the book in the planning stage; so did Terry Palmer, who publicized it on the inside cover of the firm's adult catalogue for fall 1998, a year ahead of its publication date. I also want to thank Lynne Missen for her thoughtful copy edit, and Howard Collum for his help with the index.

This book was *not* put together like a Canadian cabinet, with representatives from various constituencies. In its early stages, authors who were invited to write for it were all well-known Canadian children's authors who had experienced the events of the war years. As the wide range of their experiences became apparent, I endeavoured to broaden it even further, within the original parameters: a good story well told, written for this book, based on first hand experience.

There are many other tales. Those of us who have worked on this book hope it prompts thousands of personal stories, where younger folk ask and older folk tell their own tales of those days, and preserve their heritage of World War II for friends and family. I am collecting stories for a second volume which will complement *Too Young to Fight.*

Priscilla Galloway

PRISCILLA GALLOWAY

"My mother is not a lady," I said, with conviction.

"She is so!" Our maid, Emily, jerked upright like a startled bird. Her triangular, sharp-featured face fixed on me, black eyes bulging under her pointed cap. She lifted the silver card tray and polished its glittering circular surface again with a tea towel. "Today is her 'At Home' day. Nobody else has 'At Home' days, only ladies. Everybody knows that!" Emily bent again to check the tea wagon. "Have I got enough cups here? Ten, ummm. Sugar cubes, tongs . . ."

"Lady Macbeth was a lady," I interrupted. "Mummy is Mrs. Peebles, she's not Lady anything."

"Miss Know-It-All," said Emily bitterly, "have it your own way." This hurt. Emily gave in, but she had paid no attention to my argument. If this was victory, there was no pleasure in it.

"Emily," I asked, "can I pass the cream and sugar?"

"I expect you *can* pass the cream and sugar." Mother's high heels tapped across the polished hardwood floor. I turned towards her voice, warned by the unfortunate emphasis on "can."

"Mummy, *may* I?" The words rushed out.

"No, Priscilla Anne, you may not." My face fell. I blinked back tears.

The air was sweet with Mother's perfume. She smiled at me, and the dark world brightened. "You may pass the napkins," she said.

The chimes sounded on Mother's seven-day glass-sided clock. Her fiancé in New Zealand had given it to her before he went away to England to study, before he died of a ruptured appendix and she went to New York to study and met Dad, long before I was eight years old and we lived in Victoria and every third Tuesday, Mother was "At Home" to callers from 2 to 4 p.m. I loved that clock and its romantic story. I loved the bone china teacups, all different patterns and shapes. I loved the teapot, the matching cream and sugar and hot water jug, even though they were not pure silver, only silver plate.

Emily Jones, our "very good maid."

That must have been almost the end of the "At Home" days, though, and of maids like Emily, that spring of 1939. Before the end of the year, we would wonder why anything as frivolous as a tea party had ever seemed important.

Mother's wonderful perfume was Nuit Bleu, by Guerlain. Dad had brought a huge crystal flagon of it back from Paris in 1938. He had brought dolls wearing bright beaded costumes from Norway for me and my two younger sisters. Dad knew when he came back to Canada, after travelling on business in Czechoslovakia, France, and Scandinavia, that war would come.

We were not a rich family, although to Emily I'm sure we seemed wealthy. Mother and Dad saved for more than a decade before they could afford to buy a house. Early in 1939, we moved to Mother's dream home on Ten Mile Point, overlooking Cadboro Bay. We gathered around the radio in the living room there to hear our king, George VI, read in his slow voice Britain's declaration of war, on September 3, 1939. A few days later, our Canadian declaration followed.

"This is the first time your country has declared war," Dad told us. "In your lifetime, you girls will see Canada change from a colony into a nation. You can be very proud to be Canadian." I straightened my back, already feeling a surge of pride.

As soon as war was declared, Dad went to join the army. He came home fuming. "They won't take me," he announced in disgust. "I wrecked my eyes studying, so now I can't fight Hitler. Let it be a lesson to you, Priscilla: take care of your eyes!" Like many other intellectuals, Dad hated violence, but by then he could see no alternative. Hitler — and Nazi Germany — had to be stopped.

Dad always smoked more heavily when he was stressed; now the air was blue around him.

"What else can you do to help?" asked Mother, always practical.

Dad snorted, but the Sixteenth Scottish Regiment in the reserves was happy to let him join up as a second lieutenant, in spite of his thick glasses. Our king, George VI, wrote to say so, in an elegant document commissioning "our trusty and well-beloved" Allon Peebles, sealed with a great round blob of red wax almost as wide as the page. "How do you know the king?" I asked. Dad always told me everything. Why hadn't he told me about being a friend of the king?

Dad shrugged modestly, but his eyes shone with delight. "I don't know the king," he said, "and the king doesn't know me. Every officer gets a commission like this, but it feels as if he knows he can count on me."

The army, even the reserve army, carried an aura of splendour. Dad went off three nights a week to drill, smart in his khaki summer uniform,

Far right, Allon Peebles, 2nd Lieutenant, 3rd Battalion, Sixteenth Scottish Regiment, parading through Victoria.

swagger stick tucked under his arm. He did not read to me in the evenings anymore, and he seldom burst into a recitation of "You Are Old, Father William," or "The Wreck of the Julie Plante," or any of the other poetry he knew and had declaimed with gusto. Indeed, most evenings he wasn't home until after I was in bed. I was proud of him. I was also horribly lonely.

In November, Emily went home to get married. She came from a village up the Island where the fences were festooned with hunks of raw wool waiting to be carded, spun, and knit into the lanolin-rich sweaters that are still a West Coast Native trademark. For the past four years, I had spent more time with Emily than with my mother, who was President of the Morning Music Club and busy turning Victoria into the musical mecca of the West. Emily was not a friend or a confidant. She did not pay much attention to me, but she was home when I arrived after school, and she didn't mind if I chattered while she worked. There was a hole in my life after Emily left.

My first contribution to the war effort was learning to wash the dinner dishes and to dry the glasses without streaks. The bits of soap we used never dissolved well; the wash water was scummy and greasy. For the time being, little else changed, though change was in the air.

Dad's work took him to Ottawa in December 1940 as the first Executive Director of the Unemployment Insurance Commission. The rest of us were to stay in Victoria until the end of the school year. Mother went about selling our home with its pond and its huge bullfrog, the rhododendrons and the moss rose, the sunken garden and the wild garden where I liked to climb into my favourite oak tree to read. It was years before she let us know how much it hurt.

Mother would miss her friends when she left Victoria, though many of them were also preparing to go elsewhere. The move was easier for me. I was already a loner, finding the company of books or of wild places more congenial than that of other children. Separation from Dad was traumatic for me; leaving Victoria was not. My sisters bonded with Mother, but I had always been Daddy's girl. I did not yet know how much I would miss my secret places: the dark passage under the eaves where I could creep with my flashlight and my book; the oak tree; and the tiny island that could only be reached for half an hour at low tide.

Early in July 1941, Mother, my two sisters, and I set out for the nation's capital.

We all had new outfits for travelling. My sisters wore Liberty print dresses, princess style, made by the clever seamstress who had

Separation from Dad was traumatic for me; leaving Victoria was not. My sisters bonded with Mother, but I had always been Daddy's girl.

created the blue lace evening gown with the little sleeves that went over Mother's shoulders for a dinner party, but were detached for a ball, leaving only ultra-narrow straps. Mother was lucky it was such an elegant costume; nobody had new evening clothes until after the war. But then, they weren't much needed; there were no balls. My dress was store-bought, with bows and lace trimming its tiny heart-shaped pockets. In that dress, I could *almost* see my outsized, uncoordinated self as dainty and feminine. I had my first pair of grown-up shoes, open-toed beige canvas with a blue one-inch heel! I tottered along the decks of the *Princess* vessel that took us from Vancouver Island to the mainland, but strode confidently when the porter showed us to our compartment on the Canadian National train, having by then gotten the hang of walking in heels.

Already a budding writer, I spent many hours en route with pen and notebook, lulled by the clack of the wheels and the rocking rhythm of the great train, snuffling the gritty air. The linen handkerchiefs I had hemstitched (badly) were blackened when I blew my nose; the flowers on my new dress acquired an added random design from flecks of soot.

In no time, we arrived in Ottawa.

"My girls!" Could my father actually be crying? Maybe we all were crying.

"Little Bear" (his pet name for Mother), "Tommy" (Tommy Turkey, would you believe, his pet name for me!), "Jane" (my middle sister, named for Dad's aunt), "and can this be Noeline? What a big girl, we can't call you little Noeline anymore!" Every name was accompanied by a big hug and one of Dad's slobbery kisses. My four-year-old sister beamed as he swung her up in his arms.

"Come along," he said. "I'm taking my girls out for dinner, and then we're going home." He took my hand, and my world felt safe again.

"Home" that summer of 1941 was the family residence of General Sir Sam Hughes, who had been Canada's war minister in World War I. I leaped at the chance to sleep in the general's cavernous bedroom, which dwarfed an outsized mahogany wardrobe, dresser and nightstand, a seven-foot rolltop desk — and the crimson-canopied four-poster bed. If the mattress had been level, half a dozen people could easily have slept on it sideways; however, it sagged like a hammock in the middle; when I crept in, the mattress rose up on both sides, threatening to engulf me.

"Do you really want to sleep here?" Mother asked doubtfully. "There are enough bedrooms for all of us without using this one."

"I'll be fine," I asserted loudly. In my head, a small voice whispered, "Pride goeth before destruction, and a haughty spirit before a fall." I was a stubborn and obstinate child, constitutionally averse to admitting my own errors of judgment, even after two sleepless nights in the general's bedroom, where shadows moved in the darkness and the night air was alive with little cries.

"Mice in the walls, I expect," said Mother, "or squirrels, maybe. Of course, the draperies sway in the breeze at night when the window is open. Are you ready to move?"

"No." I wrote little mind-stories, with myself as heroine. Eventually I slept well, except for missing the sound of the sea like an ache all through me. In Ottawa, there was no cure for that.

In mid-August we moved to Westboro, where my parents had bought a solid, two-storey yellow brick home with a double lot. That fall, Dad turned over sod for the Victory garden we would plant the following spring, but in 1941 we had to buy our winter supply of carrots, potatoes, and onions, layering them with sand in the cold cellar bins. In later years, the upper shelves would gradually be filled with Mother's jars of pallid strawberries and pears, glowing raspberries, golden peaches, and crimson spiced crabapples, not to mention bread and butter pickles, mustard pickles and dills, quince jelly, gooseberry jam, and a plenitude of other jams, jellies, and conserves. That fall, they were mostly empty, because of our move. Sugar was already in short supply. Coupon rationing had not yet arrived, but nobody was supposed to use more sugar than in previous years. Mother used almost no sugar in the fruit she canned.

Our "new" house was forty years old, spacious and comfortable, though no match for the jewel we had left. My parents sold the house in Victoria for the same price they had paid, $10,400. They paid $8,800 for the house in Ottawa. Dad had treated me as a grown-up since I could remember; he thought I should know grown-up details like that. The extra money came in handy for a new stove and washing machine, a Heintzman upright, and Oriental carpets to hide the wide, unfinished softwood plank centres of our new living-room and dining-room floors. New appliances were hard to find, since all the factories had been converted to war production.

There wasn't much entertainment for civilians. My parents and some neighbours formed a folk dance group, taking turns to go to one another's homes. When it was our turn, we rolled up the carpets and moved furniture into the conservatory or against the walls, pushing the heavy floor polisher back and forth over — what? Lumps of something, not wax, I think. Borax? Talc? The resulting surface was wonderfully slippery.

I had classmates to dance only once that I remember, in grade nine or ten. I had a new record, "ABCDEFGH, I've Got a Gaaaaal in Kalamazoo," one of those you can't get out of your head. The party would have been fun if I could have relaxed a bit, but I was too nervous: there were BOYS.

How I longed for an older brother, so that I could know what those strange creatures were all about. I was frozen in their presence. In the academic world I was confident and comfortable; part of me loved showing off in class. But put me with a BOY and my throat constricted. I sat tongue-tied beside Phil in the high school orchestra for three years; in the fourth year Marilyn moved in and at once they were whispering and giggling together. I stopped taking violin lessons soon afterwards. Lucky for Marilyn that envy does not kill!

The war brought me my older brother in 1942, when cartoonist Les Callan moved in. By that time the housing shortage in Ottawa was acute; every family had to register an unused room, which would then be rented. Our spare room was the largest bedroom in the house, with the only double bed. My room was tiny; my sisters shared theirs.

Mum and Dad could have given each of us her own room, but I'm sure they never even considered doing that. My parents always knew what was right, and they were determined to do it. My sisters and I had to do it, too. This wasn't a big thing, when so many people were risking their lives. Dad likely had a say in selecting his tenants; Les and his successors fitted right in.

Les was twenty years older than I was and bald; I did not learn much about boys from him, though he endeared himself to me by brotherly acts that included disentangling a bat that got caught in my hair one scary night. Les was in the army, and his chief ambition was to be sent overseas with *The Maple Leaf*, the magazine of Canada's armed forces. As a civilian, he had been the political cartoonist for the *Toronto Daily Star*, so he was well established in his profession. He had a lovely, quirky sense of humour. Like my dad, Les had to wear glasses. His eyesight was not bad enough to keep him out of the army, but it was bad enough to keep him in Canada.

"Self portrait" by cartoonist Lieutenant F.L. (Les) Callan, from my old autograph book.

Within a year, Les had been fitted with a new invention: contact lenses. Unlike the soft lenses of today, the originals were hard and huge, approximately two centimetres in diameter. Made of glass, they were difficult to insert and must have been abominably painful to wear.

Les was determined to get posted overseas; he kept putting the lenses into his red and weeping eyes until at last the army decided he could manage without his glasses, and 1943 saw him off to Europe. His letter of December 21, 1944, to "Dear Sis Priscilla" thanks me for my Christmas parcel of underwear, a welcome change from army issue which, he wrote, "are wooly and thus itchy, so, I have yours (I mean mine) on now."

This story has jumped way ahead of itself. In September 1941, the Peebles family was still getting settled in the new house, the girls starting at a new school. I began in grade seven, but moved at Christmas to grade eight. I spent many school hours helping out in the school office, using the jelly duplicating machine or answering the phone. There was no school secretary.

This rather solitary life suited me, but it did not help me to find friends. I was very unsure of myself. Probably my classmates thought me unbearably snooty. The principal, Mr. Cameron, also taught grade eight; he made sure my work in the office did not interfere with my studies. He and his wife were members of the neighbourhood folk dance group.

Private places for wandering or reading were hard to find in wartime Ottawa. Surrounded by people, I tried to create a group where I might fit in, the Purple Hand Club (the name was supposed to suggest a secret Sicilian organization). There were four members. I composed mysterious messages, signed with an inky palm print, and persuaded the others to sneak out after bedtime to tack them to telephone poles two and three blocks away. The club was a short-lived and unsuccessful effort. It had no focus, and enthusiasm waned even before the biting November winds ended our outdoor forays. For me, the overall effect was to reinforce my generalized feelings: I was and would always be an outsider.

Christmas that first year in Ottawa was memorable. Other people may remember Christmas 1941 because the United States had entered the war earlier that month, after the Japanese attack on Pearl Harbor. For me, however, it was the Christmas of chocolate bars.

None of us had seen a chocolate bar for years. Ships, trains, and planes moved troops, weapons, and ammunition, or supplies, or raw materials for industry, whatever was needed for the war. Chocolate was not essential. Candy factories, like every other kind of factory, were converted to war production. For civilians, there were no new appliances, no new cars, not even new tires, and not much gasoline; there were certainly no chocolates.

It was my patriotic duty to be cheerfully resigned. Alas, I was a chocoholic candy monster. I felt deprived. Thoughts of other absent treats made me gloomy, too. Salted soybeans did not taste like peanuts. Chewy semi-dried banana strips were too sweet (even for me), and were a poor substitute for bananas, though better than nothing when you could get them.

On Christmas day of 1941, Cousin Anna gave me a Neilson's dark chocolate almond bar. My sisters got a milk chocolate bar each. Pre-war chocolate!

Cousin Anna got a huge hug whose intensity seemed to surprise her. I retired to a corner to gloat over her gift, sliding the silver package slowly out of its royal blue wrapper. It looked like chocolate. It felt like chocolate. But it did not smell like chocolate. It smelt like Mother's wardrobe trunk.

All three chocolate bars came out the minute our cousin left. "Mothballs," sniffed Mother, wrinkling her nose. "They've been in a trunk with mothballs." Cruel mother, she laughed and laughed.

"Maybe the smell will pass off," I suggested hopefully.

"Maybe." Dad didn't find it so funny, but Anna was *his* relative.

I nibbled. The look was chocolate. The taste was mothballs. Mother threw out the remains before I could nibble any more.

Happily, I was not deprived of books. That would have been totally unbearable. Few new books of fiction were published in Canada, since paper was needed for essentials like ration coupons and recruiting posters. Almost no books arrived from Britain. Booksellers always seemed to have a good stock of classics, however; and the second-hand market flourished. Christmas 1941 brought me *The Princess Elizabeth Gift Book*, published in Britain to raise money for a children's hospital sponsored by the Princess who is now the Queen.

The war forced me into working with other people; it socialized me. As a Girl Guide, I helped out at the local orphanage. At school I became secretary of the Red Cross Club. I baby-sat, freeing parents. I wrote to Les, to three other servicemen overseas, and to Jane Howells, my Girl Guide pen pal in Wales. I collected waste paper for our guide company's salvage drive. Sometimes a few paperback books were discarded. Naturally, they could not go to destruction unread! I developed speed-reading skills, knowing that as soon as the garage and the back porch were full of paper, stacked and tied in bundles, Mother would call the truck to pick it up.

Jane Howells, my Girl Guide pen pal in England.

Half a dozen science-fiction novels were salvaged to my shelves, though I suffered torments of guilt. Some patriotic Canadian had given that pulp fiction to be shredded for our country! By saving the books (all right, stealing them), I had sabotaged the war effort. On the other hand, it had to be wrong to throw out books, especially mesmerizing tales like these! Although the war had forced me out of my loner shell, I needed time to dream.

The Commonwealth Air Training Plan brought new friends to my family and a new element to my socialization. In Canada, we trained air crew from all over the world, in facilities all over the country; it was a major contribution to victory. The plan was organized, however, in Ottawa, and senior air force officers from Commonwealth countries were stationed there.

My mother was a New Zealander, and our home became a drop-in centre for Royal New Zealand Air Force officers, "Tiny" White and Tony Brown among them. Group Commander Tiny White was not much more than five feet tall; his wife Anne towered above him. They were an amiable couple, but I puzzled over them: how could they possibly be happy together? Their appearance was a joke!

Flight Lieutenant Tony Brown was taller than I was and did not have a senior rank to intimidate me. He had been at the fall of Singapore and had been part of a long, desperate forced march by men determined not to become Japanese prisoners of war. I thought this splendidly romantic and could not understand why Tony did not want to talk about his adventures.

Like many men, Tony disliked shopping. I was delighted to spend his money and scoured stores for gifts for his mother in New Zealand and his sister in London, who had been bombed and lost everything.

One afternoon Tony took me to a movie. This counted as a date, a serious business involving serious preparation. My girlfriend Dale came over to help me apply liquid leg makeup, the fashion industry's answer to the wartime disappearance of silk stockings.

The ads made the process look easy. The ads lied.

One began by applying Neet. ("Wash away unsightly hair from legs, armpits, and forearms. Leaves the skin smooth, white, and pleasantly scented.") My unsightly hair, wiped off with toilet paper and partly dissolved in white cream, clogged the toilet, requiring an exciting few minutes with the plunger. After Neetening, though, my legs were as smooth as if they had been sanded.

The next trick was to get the liquid mud of the makeup rubbed on evenly. This proved impossible. Even with Dale's help, my legs dried streaky. In the advertisements, a glamour girl completed the job by leaning down to draw an imitation stocking seam down the back of her leg. That looked easy, too. Another lie.

I did my hair like Veronica Lake (flipped under at the ends, with a bang hiding my right eye).

"Very nice, dear," said Mother doubtfully.

"You'll ruin your eyes," grumbled Dad.

Did I look romantic, sexy, and grown-up? Were all the girls jealous of me, standing on the streetcar arm in arm with a deeply tanned New Zealand Air Force flight lieutenant with a bushy moustache and a thousand-carat grin? People did stare at us, certainly. I remember that.

When Tony's training was accelerated, he knew that casualties in Bomber Command must have been unusually high, and that he would soon be on a ship bound for England. (He did survive the war, but was sent home to New Zealand for discharge; he never visited Canada again.)

On his last visit, Tony gave me a thick hardbound book. The first forty or fifty of its lined pages contained his aircraft recognition notes, with pencil sketches or magazine photos of various aircraft. Among them were three photos of famous paintings of nude women, each labelled like an airplane: "Hurri" (for Hurricane); "Messy" (for Messerschmitt) and "Recco," perhaps for Reconnaissance. Tony thought this was screamingly funny. So did I, though at thirteen I was shocked, not at the nudity, but at the fact that anybody dared to put something funny among notes that were to be marked. I was careful not to show these works of art to my mother, or to any of my friends at school.

Hundreds of lined pages in Tony's book were unused.

"What will you do with it?" he asked me. "Something special, I hope."

It was very special. I began copying quotations onto those pages, things I read or heard: a motley collection, mostly serious but interspersed with funny bits, word bites I wanted badly enough to take the trouble to write them down. After a year or two, I began to date each entry. I had never heard of a Commonplace Book, but mine now covers more than half a century of my life. It's probably the first possession I'd rescue in a fire.

I copied a parody of the twenty-third psalm into my book during the summer of 1944, around the time of my fourteenth birthday. In the slanguage of the time, "zombies" were conscripts, men who did not join up voluntarily but who had been drafted into the army. Only volunteers were sent overseas; conscripts did their military service in Canada, and were ridiculed for doing so, more and more bitterly as the war dragged on. Pressure mounted to send conscripts overseas, and the federal government changed the law that had exempted them in the fall of 1944, after getting a mandate to do so in a national referendum. This anonymous parody shows how many people felt:

ZOMBIE PSALM

Mackenzie King is my shepherd. I shall not wander.

He maketh me not to wear a "G.S." [General Service badge]. He leadeth me not across the still waters; he restoreth his vote. He leadeth me along the paths of Canada for his Party's sake.

Yea, though I move about from one camp to another I will fear no draft, for "King" is with me. His government and his cabinet, they comfort me.

He prepareth a table before me in the presence of mine Active enemies. He does not clip my hair too short; my glass runneth over with Canadian beer.

Surely the government will not alter its policy at this late date,
But I shall dwell within the confines of Petawawa
Forever.

Amen.

Although I was intellectually precocious, in many other areas I was dangerously naive. Having skipped two grades, I was two years younger than my classmates.

Students who cannot read develop coping strategies to mask their academic ignorance. I developed strategies to mask my lack of street smarts.

After one afternoon of five-pin bowling, I sat with some classmates and talked over soft drinks. I started to tell about our family holiday tenting at Lac Philippe.

"I'd rather have a week on Veronica Lake!" one of the fellows interrupted, with a smirk.

"Naugh-*tee*!" Beside me, Dale rolled her expressive eyes.

I smirked and rolled my eyes, too, despite my confusion. Lac Philippe was a lake. Veronica Lake was a person. *What* were they talking about? Somehow I knew they'd never stop laughing at me if I asked.

My wartime experiences threw me into the company of adult men, sometimes very powerful men. (Dad introduced me to the Prime Minister, Mr. Mackenzie King, one day, when we found ourselves descending in the same elevator at the Parliament Buildings.) Young men, in comparison, seemed to belong to a different planet; their concerns seemed trivial, their language banal. But if grown men had been less present in my life, I might have learned to talk to males my own age.

In grade eleven, however, I actually found one boy I could talk to: Bob Rosewarne, a fine artist then in grade thirteen. Bob became my steady boyfriend. I wonder now if he was as surprised as I was.

You had to have a boyfriend to go dancing at Britannia, at the far end of the streetcar line, on Friday and Saturday nights. Britannia was glamorous. We high-school girls rubbed shoulders (literally) with men in uniform. We did not trade partners much, but a few times I danced with Bob's older brother

In grade eleven, Bob Rosewarne became my steady boyfriend. I wonder now if he was as surprised as I was.

Harry, his air force blue-grey uniform rough against my cheek.

I was fourteen that year, in grade eleven. Bob was the fattest boy at school. We suited each other: oddballs both.

Bob's sausage fingers carved intricate linoleum plates for multi-coloured prints, and puppet heads for my first (and only) three-act play, a fantasy set in an alien world remotely akin to the Middle Ages. Freeel [with three "e"s] was the hero of my play. I saw him as an Errol Flynn kind of prince, but Bob carved him stylized, long-faced, with a down-turned arrogant mouth.

The night Bob asked me to go steady, he gave me his ring, a square aqua-coloured piece of glass set in silver. It fitted his baby finger, but hung loose on the ring finger of my left hand. The girls oohed and aahed over it as if it had been a diamond. This was my passport, at last, to being accepted in high school society: my twin liabilities of youth and brains were overcome by this bit of glass.

By Christmas 1944, the tide had turned in Europe. My parents always had a big party on New Year's Eve, and that year Mother doubled her recipe for Athol Brose, her New Year's specialty, and the house was redolent of its rich aroma of Scotch, honey, oatmeal, and cream. More than forty people trooped out into the snow to bring in twigs from the bushes, our hearth offering for good fortune in the year ahead.

Bob made me a chrome ring, heart-shaped, for Valentine's Day. His weight would probably have kept him out of the army, but now it looked as if he might not need to volunteer. His good friend George, a wizard on the snare drums, had joined up in time for the invasion and got a bullet in his shoulder; he would never make it into the big bands now. Bob had worried more about injuring his hands than getting killed, if he had to fight.

At school, we continued to sell war savings stamps on Friday afternoons, the way we had for years. I tried to buy at least one stamp each week. Sixteen stamps purchased one four-dollar certificate, with the government's promise to pay five dollars in seven and a half years. Most of my baby-sitting money went into stamps, though my business declined drastically when I started dating Bob.

At 11:30 on the morning of May 8, everyone at school was summoned to an assembly. The auditorium doubled as a gym, and the assembly had been called so suddenly that the folding chairs had not been set up. We knew, even before the principal called us to order: Germany had surrendered. The war in Europe was over. We had won. School was dismissed.

Bob caught up to me in the cheering crowd. My home was a block away, his a half block farther, near the streetcar tracks. "I'll call for you after lunch," said Bob. "Will your folks let you go downtown with me?"

I have no memory of the discussion, but Mother must have agreed, or I would certainly have remembered the discussion afterwards. Practising for my future career in journalism, I wrote my impressions of downtown Ottawa on that historic day: the cold wind blowing off the river; the Carillon concert, with the bells singing songs of triumph; ticker tape and toilet paper floating down from office windows. *Toilet paper!* How dared they waste it?

Sparks Street was pandemonium, packed almost solid with people dancing, singing, screaming, forming little circles that spun around a girl or two and then caterpillared off again. Protected by Bob's meaty arm, I laughed and sang and screamed as loudly as the rest.

Suddenly, I was torn loose. A sailor swung me up in his arms and spun around towards Confusion Square. I saw Bob's head, then lost him.

"Put me down!"

"Kiss me, and I'll put you down."

Would he? He smelled disgustingly of cigarettes and whiskey. It was a very quick kiss, but he did put me down. A circle of men formed around me now, hands locked together, laughing at my panic. "No!" I launched myself at two linked arms and broke through, struggling upstream against the human surge, screaming now with purpose: "Bob! Bob!"

"Anne!" He liked to call me by my middle name. Dear Bob.

VE Day, May 8, 1945: Victory at last! Celebrations spilled into the streets throughout the Allied World.

Now, half a century later, it is the intensity that I remember best, not only of that day, but of those years: the focused energy of people united by one great purpose. My grandchildren have never experienced it. The closest they might have come would be in the intensity and fervour around the Québec referendum in 1995, the "almost" one — but that was brief. In war, the intensity and effort continued for almost six years.

For me, VE Day was the climax. Great and terrible events took place afterwards, but I had no part in them. I scarcely remember VJ Day, in August, perhaps because it was summer, the quiet season, perhaps because in Ottawa the energy of rejoicing had been spent.

Some people got richer during the war; others got poorer. My family was one of those. Dad applied for raises for many members of his staff, but never for himself. Officially, wages and prices were controlled, so it should not have made a difference, but it did; most controls eroded gradually over time. Like many men, Dad worked himself unmercifully. He did not give his life, but he gave his health: it is no coincidence that he suffered his first heart attack within the first post-war year, soon after his forty-sixth birthday. Among its other effects, that heart attack destabilized my family's finances, throwing me on my own resources at the age of seventeen.

Unlike many families in those years, ours survived. I had two male cousins of fighting age, one in the army and one in the air force. Both saw action; neither was wounded. We were fortunate.

We had no television then to bring atrocities into our homes, but I had little trouble imagining horror. Les Callan's letters described scenes I had already painted in my mind. "The land of Hitler," he had written in March 1945, "is a blighted land. War has come home to roost with a vengeance! Some towns are destroyed completely (as completely as were some little Norman villages not long ago). The trees are splintered and uprooted by shells and mortars and some are blown clear out of the ground by the mighty bombs . . . . We are hopeful that the end will not be too long now," the letter continued, "but we are also wary lest some last desperate tricks are played on us. We are keeping our respirators handy." Poison gas, mustard gas that destroyed the lungs, had been outlawed after World War I, but Germany had used it then and might use it again. To our soldiers who were fighting on Hitler's own territory, it must have been a fearful possibility.

My pen pal Jane in England wrote to me on May 16, 1945, just after VE Day. "Excuse the disgusting remnant of an envelope," she began. She had glued paper over an old envelope and re-used it: a palimpsest. Her letter rejoiced: "My two cousins and a friend were liberated from the notorious Stalag-Luft III" (a German prison camp where some prisoners of war had been known to be shot, so a great anxiety to those whose dear ones were interned there).

In her town of Bishop's Castle, "everyone hung out flags and bunting. We have a Union Jack and a Welsh Dragon floating outside our house at this moment. Unfortunately many people became dead-drunk and littered the streets. At the fair everything was free and the rides lasted twice as long as usual. (I'm writing tighter to save paper as this is the last piece and we can't get any more decent.) At 11.00 p.m. there was a bonfire and fireworks. No-one had seen fireworks since 1939 when they all had to be given in to the Police who re-distributed them again last week . . . ."

Would I have joined the armed forces myself if I had been a few years older?

I am a peaceable person. Those, however, were not peaceable times. I believed that we were fighting for our survival, and for the survival of civilization. I'm a sucker for the concept of the greater good, and did not then know how variously that concept may be defined. I would have volunteered proudly, if I had not been too young to fight.

Ladies volunteered for the Morning Music Club or the Red Cross, not for the services. Emily had been right all those years ago; Mother was that kind of lady. I was not.

PRISCILLA GALLOWAY *became a garbage collector, cucumber farmer and scuba diver, as well as a professor, educational consultant and proud author of twenty books. An innovative designer of English curriculum for gifted students, she pioneered inclusion of current Canadian literature. A writer all her life, Priscilla became a full-time author in 1993. Her fascination with ancient Greece is reflected in* Daedalus and the Minotaur, *three other novels in her Annick series, and* Snake Dreamer *(Stoddart Kids). Priscilla's books have been shortlisted for the Canadian Library Association Young Adult Book of the Year, and for the Mr. Christie's Book Award.* Truly Grim Tales *appears on two American Library Association Honor Lists. Priscilla is a past president of Ontario Council of Teachers of English and of CANSCAIP (the Canadian Society of Children's Authors, Illustrators and Performers); the Queen's Alumnae Marty Award helped to finance her Ph.D. studies.* Too Young to Fight *is her most complex literary production to date, and most thrilling.*

JANET LUNN

This isn't really a story. It's a collection of memories about a few years in my life.

They were years that were very important in the world, the years between 1939 and 1945 when World War II was being fought. If you were writing a history book about those years, the part of the world where I lived might not even be in it. But if you were writing a book about the world's ordinary people during that extraordinary time, my family and my friends and I might be some of the people you would put in it.

I am an old woman now and there have been many wars, terrible wars, since 1945 but I still think of the one that ended that year as *the war*. We all do, those of us who were around then — even those of us who lived in North America where it did not affect us the way it did people in Great Britain or Europe or Asia. We were not invaded, we were not bombed, we did not go hungry or, where I lived, have to leave our homes. I did not have brothers who went off to fight. We were three girls in our family — Martha, Ann, and I — with one brother, Frank, who was three when the war began in Europe.

The war began for Canada and the rest of the British Commonwealth when the German army invaded Poland in 1939 and Great Britain and France declared war on Germany. The United States didn't get into the war until the Japanese bombed the American naval base at Pearl Harbor in Hawaii in 1941. By that time, the British, the Commonwealth countries, and the French, called the *Allies*, were fighting the Germans and the Italians, called the *Axis*. The Japanese had invaded China in 1937 and were trying to take over most of the rest of Southeast Asia. When the United States declared war on Japan the day after the bombing of Pearl Harbor, the *Allies* followed suit. The *Axis* Powers then joined with Japan and declared war on the United States. By the time the *Axis* countries had overrun Holland, Belgium, France, and all of Eastern Europe but Yugoslavia, the Soviet Union had joined the *Allies*. The war had become truly a world war.

Mother with Martha, Ann, Frank, and me — 1940.

I lived in the United States in 1941, not far from New York City. I was thirteen when the war started for us. It was the seventh of December, a cold, bleak Sunday afternoon. We were in our car, driving home from visiting my grandmother, and we heard the news on the car radio. At least, that's the way I remember it. My sister Martha remembers that we heard it in my grandmother's apartment at the college where she worked. I hate to tell her so but I think Martha is right because not many cars had radios in those days and, when I think about it, I'm sure our little black Willys sedan didn't have one. I do remember that we talked about the Pearl Harbor bombing all the way home and that we kids were so full of questions we almost didn't notice that the car heater didn't work. Would the United States go to war? Would we be bombed? Would Dad have to fight? Would we have to leave home the way the English children had? Where would we go?

The next day President Roosevelt answered one of our questions. He declared war on Japan.

The war had been part of our lives for as long as I could remember. Even though I was a very small child when Hitler came to power in Germany in 1933, I remember hearing his speeches over the short-wave radio in the living room of the farmhouse in Vermont where we lived then. My great-grandmother, who lived just across our side yard in a cottage attached to the barn, always came in the evenings to listen to the speeches. She was a person to speak her mind very plainly and she had only listened to Hitler's first speech for a few minutes when she said in a contemptuous tone of voice, "low German." Only she didn't say "low German," she said it in German, "platt deutsch."

I don't actually remember hearing her say "platt deutsch" when she first heard Hitler speak; my mother told me about that years later. I do remember my great-grandmother being in our living room, listening to the speeches and I sure remember the tone of voice she used when she was disgusted by something. She was an imposing woman, tall and big, with a strong, square face, bright blue eyes, and beautiful white hair. I was always a little afraid of her. I remember thinking that Hitler wouldn't shout so much if Ohma would, just once, pinch her sharp blue eyes at him the way she did at us sometimes.

My great-great-great grandparents on both sides of my family had all come to the United States from Germany back in the 1840s, and, until our generation, everyone in both families still spoke both German and English. We children spoke only English. Some of our customs were still German, though. We always had our Christmas stockings on St. Nicholas Day, the sixth of December, and our Christmas celebration on Christmas Eve. Our aunts were called *tante*, our uncles, *onkel*, and they had German names like Mechtildis and Franz. My mother's name was Margarethe, my father's was Hermann. Our great-grandmother we called *Ohma*, the German word for grandmother, but we called our two grandmothers, Grandma, and our one grandfather, Grandpa.

In those early years I don't remember anything the grown-ups said about Hitler, the Nazis, or their rise to power, but when I close my eyes, I can still see my mother and my father sitting on the living-room sofa beside the big, cathedral radio, Ohma in her chair drawn close to it. I remember that room in our Vermont farmhouse very clearly even though we moved from there when I was ten. It had dark red-and-cream flowered wallpaper and a rug patterned in squares where my sisters and I used to shoot marbles. It had a shiny, brown parlour stove near the back wall, a small chair and a big armchair with an ottoman along the side wall, and a sofa under the two front windows.

The radio stood on a table beside the sofa. The voice from it, shouting and shrieking in the language that sounded familiar but that I didn't understand, was frightening and I knew it frightened the grown-ups, too, because as they leaned into it, listening avidly, now and then they would turn to each other and say something in low, horrified tones in German.

How we kids hated being German! Our name, Swoboda, wasn't German, it was Czech (one of our father's ancestors had been Czech), and every single morning of every single day in those years, I said a prayer of gratitude that it didn't sound German — and always added another that nobody would find out that my grandmother had been called Schmelz before she'd married the Czech name and that I had relatives named Mann and Warmkessell and Schultz.

I don't think Hitler's speeches were heard over the short-wave radio once the war began in Europe, nor do I remember the beginning of the war. We moved in January 1939 to the town of Rye, New York, an hour's train ride out of New York City where my father had a new job. All my memories of that year are about that move to the busy suburban town from our Vermont farmhouse. It was agonizing. I was just ten. How could I care about Hitler, the war in Europe, or anything beyond the terrors of having to find a place for myself in a huge new school where I didn't know anybody?

But Rye was only a half hour's drive from where my father's mother lived and just over an hour from where my mother's parents and aunt lived. The relatives came for Sunday-afternoon visits almost every week. We children had to think about the war then. We had to sit there, squirming in our chairs (trying to stuff ourselves with cake and surreptitiously making faces at each other) while the grown-ups drank coffee, ate coffee cake, and endlessly talked politics. Oh the boredom of those Sunday afternoons! There were arguments, loud and long ones, about what the government was and was not doing about everything, and sooner or later the talk always turned to Hitler, the Nazis, and whether or not the United States should get into the war.

Our great-aunt, Tante Lulu, would argue with tears in her eyes (I was so embarrassed to see a woman that old crying — and about a thing like a war on the other side of the world) that we really had to help the British. "You know how Uncle Hugo felt," she would say, lowering her voice dramatically. "After all, he fought with the British in the last war." (Tante Lulu's favourite brother had been with the American Expeditionary Force serving with the British during World War I, and had died later as a result of the gassing.)

"We mustn't be hasty," my father would shake his head. My father was a fiercely patriotic American; he was also a very conservative man who didn't believe in jumping into things — not new ideas and not causes, no matter how passionately he agreed with them. "We'd better wait and see what develops. The French and the British are strong. The war won't last long. We're better out of it on this side of the world."

Then we were in the war and my father marched himself right down to the recruiting centre in our town and tried to join the navy — and was turned down. He was forty-three years old and he had arthritis and he hadn't expected that the navy would send him to sea but he was working as a designer of machinery and he had convinced himself that the navy would find him useful. In those days, however, only a person who was able to serve on active duty was accepted into a military service.

That was a dark day in our house. The United States Navy did not want my father. He sat in his big chair in the living room of our house in Rye all evening with his coffee cup in his hand, not drinking it, just sitting there, for hours. None of us had wanted him to go off and be in the navy, but we all felt terrible to see him so despondent.

Some of our teachers went off to war — and became heroes in our eyes (Mr. Walsh, the dreaded Latin teacher who threw chalk when a kid wasn't paying attention, was, suddenly, Johnny Walsh, the exciting navy captain). A couple of men on our street went. One of them, a man whose name I wish I could remember, was an officer in the army. I was thirteen and, even though he seemed old to me, I thought he looked so handsome in his uniform that I had quite a crush on him — but nothing like the crushes I had, one after the other, on the high-school boys in uniform.

I was in grade eight in 1941. We finished elementary school at the end of grade seven in Rye, so I was in high school. The kids in grade twelve, the seniors, seemed very glamorous and, when those senior boys who were already eighteen began to leave for basic training, they seemed more god-like than movie stars. Not just the boys, their girlfriends, too. We — my friend Betsy and I — would observe the girls covertly. Did they look as though they had been crying? Were they sighing softly? Were the sweaters they had on favourites of those boyfriends off at camp or overseas? We imagined them reading letters from the front lines, imagined them dripping tears onto those letters, carrying them next to their hearts.

My cousin Paul, just out of college, became a bomber pilot in the Army Air Corps. Paul was very good looking — tall and lean with dark hair and eyes. He was fun and he always had time for his younger cousins. There wasn't a woman under seventy who knew him who wasn't half in love with him. In his uniform, my sisters and I thought he was more devastatingly handsome than Tyrone Power, Van Johnson, and Glenn Ford wrapped up in one package. He went off for his training to an Air Corps base in Alabama. One day, late the next spring, he arrived home to surprise us all — not only with himself but with a wife.

Cousin Paul with my brother Frank, 1936.

It was an enormous shock for our aunt and uncle but we cousins thought it was great. Alice was blonde and pretty and she had a soft southern accent that I tried hard to imitate until Martha asked me, one day, if I had something wrong with my voice. (I didn't answer but I stopped trying to be Alice.) What's more, Paul and Alice came home in a sky-blue Cadillac convertible — and they took us kids for a ride. I could hardly contain myself. It was a warm, clear evening just at sunset. The leaves on the trees were still new and they hung over the streets like soft, green lace. We drove through those streets, the spring breeze in our faces, our hair blowing, and I felt like a princess sitting in the back seat of that breathtaking car behind the king and queen of the world.

Seven months later Paul was killed in a training accident in the sky over the Alabama training field.

He was buried in Vermont in the graveyard of our old village, high on the hill that overlooked the countryside where he'd spent all his summers and later gone to college. My mother and father went to the funeral but it cost too much money for all of us to go.

I came home from school that afternoon feeling miserable. I was late because I'd had to stay after school, the walk home seemed twice as long as usual, the old graveyard on Milton Road twice as gloomy, it was raining, and the leaves were almost all off the trees. I couldn't stop thinking about the funeral. When I got home, Martha had made cocoa. Martha is four years older than I and, when we were kids, she was sometimes quite motherly towards us younger ones (Ann is two years younger than I, and Frank is eight years younger). I was comforted by that kindness and I was all set for us to sit down and cheer ourselves up by being properly mournful together. But Martha had made the cocoa in order to keep herself busy while she thought of a way to tell me about a fresh disaster.

"I want you to sit down, Janet," she said softly — I think she got that line and also the solemn look she had on her face from a movie.

"Something's happened to your canary."

"My canary? Doc? What's happened to him?"

Here Martha's efforts to be the thoughtful, tactful big sister failed her. "He's dead," she said.

I jumped up, spilled my cocoa all over the rug, and ran across the room to where the bird cage stood by the front window. It was true. There lay my canary on his back, with his little twig legs sticking straight up in the air. His black and yellow feathers were as bright as ever but his round black eyes were not. I began to cry. Martha began to cry. When Ann came home a few minutes later, she cried.

Sniffling and snuffling, we mopped up the cocoa and went looking for something to bury the dead bird in. All we could find was a graham-cracker box. We dumped out the crackers and put a layer of Kleenex in the box. I lifted the bird out of his cage (shuddering all the while because I hate touching dead things) and put him on top of the Kleenex and closed the lid. We dug a hole in the backyard and put the cracker box into it. We smoothed over the dirt and, when we had finished, we put a small bunch of late marigolds on top. I think we said the Lord's Prayer. Then we all sat down on the ground in the rain and cried again. For the bird. For Paul. For the lonesomeness of Mother and Father having gone off to Paul's funeral without us. For all the fears about the war we could never quite talk about.

I have hazy recollections of others from our town who died or were captured in battle. There was a boy I liked in Martha's high-school graduating class who sometimes smiled at me. I felt a personal sense of betrayal when he was killed in action in France. A classmate's brother was shot down over the English Channel and our whole class mourned. A neighbour's cousin came home with both his legs gone.

But there was only one other truly horrible thing to happen to anyone close to us and it happened the same year my cousin Paul died. The American forces in the Bataan Peninsula in the Philippine Islands had been surrendered to the Japanese and forced to march fifty-five miles without food or water. Thousands of them died. An American war correspondent called it "The Death March from Bataan." News photographers took pictures of the surrender and *Life* magazine carried a large, double-page spread showing the weary, heart-sick soldiers. Our neighbour, the handsome army officer, whose name I can't remember, was among them. His wife and his children hadn't known he was in the Philippines until they saw the picture. They never heard from him again.

There are other, brighter memories. Towards the end of the war, one of the girls in my grade eleven class was going out with an air force pilot and he and his crew named their plane after her — every girl in our class was envious. My mother belonged to the navy league and we had sailors on leave from the nearby naval hospital come for weekends of home-cooked meals, but that simply did not compare with having a plane named after you.

I did volunteer work at the local hospital and felt very important and I exchanged letters with a young English soldier. I loved that correspondence. I was terribly shy and even though we weren't writing love letters, in my daydreams, Robin played the part of all the boyfriends I didn't have. I stopped writing to him when I finished high school and went off to university and I've often wished I had kept on, at least until I'd learned what became of him after the war.

Details in our lives were affected by the war, less interesting than sailors on leave or even a correspondence with a British soldier but things we all remember. We were all fingerprinted (in case we were bombed and our bodies would have to be identified) and had air raid drills in school in addition to the regular town drills. Rationing began early in the war. Gas, sugar, meat, butter, silk, paper, and a lot of other things I can't recall were rationed either because of being needed in the armed forces or because they couldn't be imported from Europe or Asia.

Margarine was new to us and it came, white as lard, in a package with a little envelope of bright orange powder that we had to stir into it so it would look more like butter. Our mother always gave that job to one of us girls and we fought as hard about who was going to be stuck with stirring the marge as we did over who had to do the dishes. My mother told us we should be grateful that we were not living in France or Belgium or Holland where the Germans had invaded or even in England where bombs were dropping every night and food was so scarce people were lucky to get one egg a week for a whole family. We wished we were living in England where there was real excitement and no margarine to colour.

Ration calendars and coupon books were issued early in the war. My mother told us we should be grateful that we were not living where food was so scarce people were lucky to get one egg a week for a whole family.

There are songs from those days I still know the tunes and (most of) the words to, popular songs like *I'll Walk Alone* and *I'll Be Seeing You,* about women longing for their lovers off fighting. There are others like *Comin' in on a Wing and a Prayer* and *American Patrol* that got us all stirred into a patriotic ardour. And the movies, the wonderful, tearful, even-more-patriotic movies! We wept and cheered over *Mrs. Miniver,* the story about the evacuation of the British soldiers from Dunkirk. We were thrilled by the spy and counter-spy movies like *Casablanca* and *The Last Time I Saw Paris,* and, although I can't bring a single one of them to mind now, there were countless movies about brave American boys in battle and I loved them all.

While we were never bombed and no submarines shot up through the waters along our shore, Rye was on Long Island Sound, an inlet of the Atlantic Ocean, and, being only thirty-two miles north of New York City, there was a very real danger that German submarines would come into the Sound. Oil slick from sunken ships did wash up onto our beach. Because our house was only a five-minute walk away, we could hear the seaplanes taking off and landing and the steady, reassuring noise of the patrol boats' engines.

There was always the danger, too, that we would be bombed. So street lights were not turned on at night, the top half of car headlights had to be painted black, and we all had to have heavy blackout curtains on our windows during air raid drills. Two air raid

Glow-in-the-dark "kutouts" included with this Blackout Kit were designed to make the nightly ritual less frightening for children.

drill incidents stand out in my memory and both of them are a little bit funny — although neither of them seemed funny at the time, not to the people they happened to.

The first has to do with my sister Martha and me. The bedroom we shared had no blackout curtains so, if we meant to be in that room during a drill, we had to have the lights out. One night, one totally black, moonless night, we were in our room when Martha's favourite radio program, *Inner Sanctum*, came on just as the air raid drill began. Out went the lights. On went the radio. *Inner Sanctum* was a mystery story, a creepy one, and it always began with the opening of a door that sounded as though it had tight, rusty hinges. Then a low, chilling man's voice would intone very slowly, "Go-o-o-o-d e-e-evening, this is Raymond, your host." The rusty-hinged door would close and the play would begin.

"Isn't this swell!" said Martha, happily settling herself on the floor by her bed in the dark.

"Yeah, swell," I said loudly. I was determined that Martha would not detect a single note of fear in my voice. At the same time, I squinched down in the pillows of my bed as close to the window as I could get so as to get the benefit of whatever light there might possibly be. I was an awfully timid kid. I hated *Inner Sanctum* and Raymond, your host, but I hated even more how Martha would make fun of me if I let on. But the second Raymond-your-host's menacing tones came on the air, I crept from my bed. I got almost to the door before Martha noticed.

"You're not going somewhere else just when *Inner Sanctum* is coming on?" She said it in that sarcastic tone of voice that always made me want to hit her.

"I . . . I have to go to the bathroom. I'll be right back." My tone of voice, I thought, was suggesting great disappointment that I had to miss a single moment of this treat.

"I'll bet you'll stay there for a whole hour, too." She wasn't giving in an inch.

So I sat there for a whole hour, in the dark, absolutely terrified and all the Nazis in Germany could have marched into my room set to torture me and I wouldn't have cared a bit if only they would rescue me from Raymond, your host. (My sister Martha does not remember any of this.)

The second incident has to do with Mr. Kinney, the dancing-school teacher who was, I think, every bit as timid as I. No, that can't be true because he volunteered to be an air raid warden, which meant patrolling in the dark to make sure every living person was off the street. I know this story because my mother was the chief warden for our neighbourhood, and all the other wardens had to report back to our house after the all-clear sounded.

Warden Headquarters: my mother was the chief warden for our neighbourhood.

Mr. Kinney's beat was out on Milton Road where the old pioneers' cemetery was. He had to patrol that stretch of ink-black road without even a flashlight. Mr. Kinney (his first name was Hubert) was a small, thin man whose eyes twitched nervously. He had dyed black hair and was probably around sixty years old. I knew him because my parents made me go to his class every Friday night to learn ballroom dancing. I never really did learn it but I can still hear Mr. Kinney's rather high, flat voice, "Children, one, two, three, four, one, two, three, four, and please, PLEASE do not jump about so!" as he tried, valiantly, to teach the waltz to us awkward thirteen- and fourteen-year-old girls and boys who would much rather have been learning to jitterbug.

Poor Mr. Kinney! The graveyard on Milton Road had in it the remains of people who had died as long ago as 1630. Almost nobody had been buried there for probably two hundred years. So there went Mr. Kinney, his protective air raid helmet on his head, nervously "hmm, hmming" to himself, pacing his beat back and forth, back and forth, when out of the graveyard came a small, quavering voice, "Is it all right for me to come out now?"

"Well!" said Mr. Kinney, when he told my mother about it as he was reporting in after the all-clear was sounded. "Mrs. Swoboda, I jumped, no, truly, I leapt, I absolutely leapt three feet in the air and I fear, I really fear I must have screeched. You can only imagine how terrified I was. But I did not run. No, I did not run. I gathered my wits about me and I stood my ground. I demanded to know who had spoken. To my relief, to my very great relief, it was Mrs. Taylor's cleaning help going home late from work. I know she did the right thing. She was following instructions to the letter. She got off the street as she was instructed but, oh, my . . ."

After Mr. Kinney and all the other air raid wardens had reported in and gone home, how we all laughed — and wondered if Mrs. Taylor's cleaning help had been as scared as Mr. Kinney. Later, when I told my friend Barbara who lived up the street and also went to dancing class, we imagined the whole scene together. Mr. Kinney, probably humming to himself, "one, two, three, four, one, two, three, four," and practising his waltz up and down the street just as the voice came out of the graveyard. How we wished it had been someone ready to tell him she'd been buried there three hundred years ago, waiting, just waiting, for the time to be right for her to come back to life.

Janet Swobada (high school graduation yearbook photo), 1946.

We moved again, in 1944, to Montclair, a town in New Jersey. I don't remember air raid drills there, or blackouts although we may have had them — maybe not, though, because we were inland and not in the same kind of potential danger. A year later, the war was over. In my last year of high school in 1946 we had returning servicemen in our classes, catching up on the schooling they had left in order to go off to war. I left that fall for university in Canada and wasn't really aware of the other changes peacetime brought. I've lived in Canada ever since and I have lost contact with old classmates and old neighbourhoods.

Those war years are a very long time ago now and my wartime memories are jumbled in my mind like photographs in a box piled up with no regard for time or importance. There are the newspaper pictures of battles and heroes, the stories of terrible deprivations in Britain and in the enemy-occupied countries, along with the girl in my high-school class who had the plane named after her, the ration books, songs, movies, radio programs, the sailors who came to us for home-cooked meals, and the air raid drills — all mixed up with our neighbour who died on "The Death March from Bataan," my cousin Paul, and the boy who came home without his legs. They're all in the same box, the one that holds my childhood and teenage years but the box is not labelled "Childhood and Teenage Years." It's labelled, "Remembering the War."

Janet Lunn *came to Canada in 1946, a year after the war ended. She attended Queen's University, married, and raised five children. She lives in Prince Edward County where most of her novels are set. She has the Order of Ontario, is a Member of the Order of Canada, and a past chair of The Writers' Union of Canada. Her novels, histories, and picture books have won most of Canada's top awards for children's literature, including the Governor General's Award for* The Hollow Tree *in 1998.*

Janet's great gift lies in her ability to bring the past alive both in her historical fiction and in her non-fiction — her history, The Story of Canada, *written with Christopher Moore, won Mr. Christie's Book Award for 1992. This memoir is new territory for her; when she told her grandson she was writing it, he said, in awed tones, "Wow, Grandma, that's history!" She was delighted.*

Dorothy Joan Harris

Most people would find it hard to pinpoint their earliest memory.

For me it's easier, because my first memory is of an earthquake that occurred in southern Japan, and its date, 1933, is in the geography books.

I can remember that afternoon quite clearly. I was sitting in the kitchen of our house in Mikage with Ohisa-san, our cook. Ohisa's own child, Ko-chan, would have been there too. When the sudden shaking began I wasn't much upset — at two years old I didn't know enough to be afraid. But I remember the sudden look of fear on Ohisa's face, and I remember how she snatched me up and ran outside. Snatched *me* up, not Ko-chan. We were far from the epicentre of the quake, so the house wasn't damaged and no one was hurt — but still, in that moment it was me that Ohisa carried to safety.

All my early memories are filled with faces like Ohisa's — kindly, caring, loving . . . and Japanese. There was Ohisa herself, who looked after me, scolded me when I misbehaved, and never tattled when I would leave our good English-style food on my plate and sneak off to her kitchen for something tastier from her Japanese-style dinner. There was Yuki, Ohisa's eldest child,

Outside our house in Mikage near Kobe, Japan, before the war started. I am the baby being held by one of our Japanese helpers. My brothers are standing in front of our Canadian grandmother who was visiting the family.

who would patiently keep me entertained, with games and origami and silhouette-cutting. And there was Mrs. Hoshino (whom we called Auntie 'No), an older woman who was my mother's closest friend in Japan, and the nearest thing to a grandmother that my brothers and I knew.

And so, when eventually we were living in Canada, a Canada that was at war with Japan, it was impossible for me to connect these gentle faces with the descriptions of cruel, ferocious Japanese soldiers that filled our news stories. I am enormously grateful that there was no television then. I didn't have to actually see the cruel faces in every evening newscast. And since I was as self-centred as most children are, the question of whether or not I might be allowed a pair of skates was much more important to me than any world news. To me, reading the newspaper usually meant reading the comics, and listening to the radio (there was only one radio in the house) meant *Baby Snooks* and *The Jack Benny Show.*

What did register on my consciousness, very strongly, was the change the war had made to our everyday style of living.

I imagine everyone plays the game of "What if . . ." For me that game asks: "What would my life have been like if there had been no war, if we'd been able to stay in our house in Mikage, if I'd grown up in that comfortable life?"

Our home there was a big two-storey house, with diamond-paned windows and polished floors (kept shining by Ohisa). Our street was called Uenoyama, which meant "top of the mountain," though, in fact, it was only partway up the mountain, one in a range of mountains that rose up from the Inland Sea behind Kobe and Osaka. The street was a short one (which made our house number, 1670, rather a puzzlement!) and our neighbours were well-to-do Japanese families, their houses hidden behind high walls or hedges, as ours was. It was an easy, happy life, and in that life I never remember money even being mentioned. It was just something that was *there* whenever I wanted a new package of origami papers or a kite or a special treat of ice cream at the big Daimaru department store in Kobe. But when that life disappeared and we were settled in a small box of a house in St. Catharines, then the pervading worry about money penetrated even my self-centredness.

I can still remember the disappointment of my first Christmas in Canada. When we left Japan we brought only necessities with us. These did not include my big doll house or any of the beautiful dolls which my father's Japanese friends had showered on me. At seven I was still of an age to want to play dolls with my new Canadian friends. So as Christmas approached I was hoping for a doll, just a small one from the Eaton's catalogue, to replace my lost beauties. We had no Christmas tree, but among the meagre pile of presents on the piano bench was a box for me. It was about the size of a small doll and when I shook it, it sounded promising.

"This will be a doll for me," I told my grandmother confidently.

This was my real Canadian grandmother, a somewhat sterner person than my Japanese "pretend" grandmother. She gave a snort. "It's something a lot more useful than a doll," she informed me. "You're too old to be playing with dolls."

Useful it undoubtedly was: a pair of slippers. And there was no doll for me.

But that was merely a child's disappointment. What I could not see, at age seven, was how hard this change in our circumstances was on my mother. In our Japanese house there were many helpers: the washerwoman who came once a week to take away all our laundry, the sewing woman who came twice a year to sew clothes for us all, Ohisa who held sway in the kitchen. Now there were no servants. My mother no longer spent the day in one of her soft silk dresses, playing the piano and giving music lessons to genteel Japanese ladies. What's more, there were chores expected of *me*: dishes to be washed, floors to be swept, and laundry to be scrubbed down in a dark, dismal basement.

For me there were compensations for our change in circumstances. In Japan I had played alone (my two brothers were much older than I was and Yuki did not always have time for me) in our walled garden. Now, in Canada, there was a whole street full of children, and I was introduced to the joys of hide-and-seek, hopscotch, and tag. Also, in Japan I had only the handful of children's books that my father's English relatives had sent out to us. Now there was the St. Catharines Public Library, with a basement area devoted entirely to children's books. What a treasure trove! I think that it was reading *The Count of Monte Cristo* nonstop that led to my first pair of glasses.

For my mother there were no such compensations, and for my father (who later joined us in Canada) I think the change in our lives was hardest of all. He was an Englishman, a professor of English at the University of Osaka. In Japan, in those days, a teacher (a *sensei*) was accorded the highest respect of any profession. I can remember walking through the village of Mikage with my father and seeing all the shopkeepers bowing respectfully to him.

And he had seen war coming. During the late thirties he, along with an American and a Canadian professor, had given some lectures at several American universities, giving warning that Japan was going to go to war, against the United States. He had also written an article in the *London Illustrated News* about this, quoting a Chinese proverb: "He who rides a tiger may find it hard to dismount." No one in the States or England paid any attention; he was simply not believed.

By 1938 it was evident to everyone that the military party in Japan was becoming ever more powerful and war-like, and many non-Japanese families were making plans to leave. My father's article in the London paper — which was not complimentary to the Japanese, implying that Japan was riding a mighty tiger in her war with China and would come off worst — *was* noticed in Japan.

My father was a professor of English at the University of Osaka.

That speeded up his own decision, that my mother and two brothers and I should leave Japan. Though I wasn't aware of it at the time, we four left Japan in rather a hurry. And perhaps it was in those hurried weeks that another memory slots into place. My brothers and I went to a Canadian school in Kobe, and one morning, on the walk from the train up the hill to our school we were stopped at a main road, unable to cross it because of a parade of marching soldiers. There was squad after squad of beige-uniformed soldiers, heading towards the dock area. When they had finally all passed we were late for school, and I rushed into my classroom full of excuses.

"I'm sorry I'm late — but we couldn't get across Motomachi Road for all the soldiers."

"Soldiers?" I remember my teacher's look of sudden alarm. "What soldiers?"

"Soldiers, a whole parade of them, all marching past. We couldn't cross the road . . . so I couldn't help being late—"

My teacher cut off my excuses then. But the worried look on her face didn't entirely disappear, I remember.

We had a sailing date for March 1938, on a Japanese freighter, the *Kinka Maru.* And we very nearly missed that date, as I inconveniently came down with mumps a few days before we were due to sail. But sail we did, the four of us. And that voyage brings back more warm memories of kindly Japanese. Since we all spoke Japanese fluently, my brothers and I soon made friends with the crew and were allowed almost everywhere on board — especially the galley where the cook could always find a treat for us. It was the *Kinka Maru*'s maiden voyage so she was freshly painted, and to this day the smell of new paint takes me back to those days.

My father, however, stayed on in Japan. He loved Japan, and he had a job there, a good one (though even with this good job the money had to be stretched very thin to cover a second household in Canada). Just how dangerous it was for him to stay on like that, I've never known, but I do remember coming upon my mother one day in our Canadian home, crying with worry over him. (This led to my writing my first poem, mercifully lost to posterity, some bit of doggerel that began: "Oh Father across the sea . . .")

But eventually, in the summer of 1941, even he left — fortunately, because any Westerners who stayed much later than that were interned for the war. And in Canada there were certainly no bowing shopkeepers and no university position. He finally found some menial office job and toiled away at it, his heart still in Japan.

And then, in December, his words of warning were proved accurate.

I remember that day, a sunny Sunday, December 7. My brother Bob was listening to our radio and shouted the news to us all that the Japanese had bombed Pearl Harbor. What I don't remember is my parents' reaction on that dreadful day — was I too self-centred to even share in their pain? At any rate there were no more letters from Auntie 'No (I still have her last letter to my mother, signed, "I remain, your loving Japanese mother, Auntie 'No"). And

My mother's last letter from Auntie 'No.

I wish I could write more and more but my head is very tired & busy so I cannot, Please pardon me and give my love to Dear Mother and Dear Children. I remain
your loving Japanese mother
Auntie 'No.

December 1st 1939.

My dear Alice,—
Just it very quickly past away, one year! I feel, in a dream, I am having 1939 Christmas again now.
I am sorry I was very busy and all the time I felt very tired so I could not ready for nicer present and card.
I posted yesterday little parcel for you all from Kobe. Please accept my heart. I hope it will arrive just in time your day!
I visited Akira's family in Tokyo beginning in November and stayed ten days. They were very well and Fujiko manageing very nicely herself, without her husband. Perhaps, you knew already about Akira. He is also very well in North of Manchuko now.

even if I didn't listen to the news very often or read the front page of the newspapers, I quickly learned that the Japanese — I had never heard the term "Japs" before — were now the enemy. Still graven in my memory is the day some schoolmates taunted me.

"You're a Jap," they shouted.

"I am not a Jap," I cried.

"Yes, you are, you were born there. You told us so."

"Being born there doesn't make me a Jap."

"It does so."

"It does *not*! I'm not a Jap!"

Eventually they left me alone.

Why did I not stand up for my Japanese friends and tell my schoolmates that there were good, kindly Japanese people, too? But I didn't. Like all children I didn't want to seem different from my classmates. I quickly forgot the Japanese words I once knew, except for a few household terms that we all still used — it was a long time before I learned any other word for chest of drawers than *tansu* or any other word for nightgown than *nemaki.*

By that December of 1941 the war in Europe had been going on for two years, and many young Canadian men were fighting there already. But it was when the United States entered the war that we all seemed to become more involved. "The war effort" was a phrase on everyone's lips, and everyone tried to do their bit.

We saved newspapers, the foil from cigarette packages and chocolate bars, and empty toothpaste tubes and tin cans. We saved all our cooking fat, too — it used to puzzle me as to how that would help the war effort, but I've since learned the fat was used in making ammunition. There were articles in magazines and newspapers telling us how to reuse and remake clothes and household items, so as to save all materials (though our household's lack of money had taught us all there was to know about making do long before this).

My mother spent afternoons rolling bandages for the Red Cross, and both she and my grandmother spent many hours knitting warm scarves and helmets and socks which the Red Cross distributed to the soldiers overseas. This knitting was easy for my grandmother, who liked to knit, but harder, I think, on my mother, whose fingers were more at home on a piano keyboard.

For today's generation probably the most remarkable thing about these war years is the wholehearted patriotism we all felt. There was none of the protests, the conscience-searching, the wavering that characterized the Vietnam war years. There were some young men, "conscientious objectors," who chose other kinds of work than fighting — and this took courage, too. But for the most part it was a patriotic war, fought "for King and country," a war that we felt had to be fought, and we will perhaps never be so united in purpose again. At church, there were special prayers about the war; at school, assemblies began with the singing of "There'll Always Be an England." There were posters everywhere: posters encouraging men to volunteer for the forces ("Your Country Needs YOU"), posters discouraging unnecessary travel ("Is This Trip Really Necessary?"), posters warning against careless talk ("Loose Lips Sink Ships") — though I couldn't imagine how anyone in St. Catharines could possibly know anything that might help the enemy, or who there could possibly be in St. Catharines who would want to help the enemy.

Even a birthday card I made for my mother, which I found recently among some old photographs, surprised me — I had decorated it not with flowers, as I would have expected, but with doves bearing the word "PEACE," and with a Union Jack carefully painted in one corner.

The birthday card I made for my mother was not decorated with flowers. Instead, I had drawn doves delivering love, joy, and peace.

We all felt this intense patriotism in spite of the fact that here in Canada we experienced no real danger or menace from the war. Back then, the Atlantic and Pacific oceans seemed a sure safeguard against any attack on our land. Though I was a child easily frightened by many things, I can remember no feeling of fear in those days. Fear came for me much later, during the Cold War, when intercontinental missiles made us all feel threatened wherever we lived, and children in classrooms were drilled in what to do in the event of a nuclear attack.

Not long after Pearl Harbor rationing came in. We didn't have a car, so the gas rationing didn't affect us. And as for food rationing — coffee and large amounts of meat weren't in our food budget anyway. (Now if they had rationed ice cream cones I would have felt it! Ice cream had been a rare treat for me in Japan, one I enjoyed only when we went to the Daimaru restaurant in Kobe. But here in Canada a nickel would get you an ice cream cone any time, and a quarter bought a brick of ice cream, which, of course, had to be eaten right away, since we had no freezer in our small refrigerator.)

My contributions towards the war effort were pretty small. Though I knew how to knit, I didn't join my mother and grandmother in making warm things for soldiers; my efforts went towards making myself the sloppy joe sweater that I desperately wanted. Occasionally I did bring my allowance of a quarter to school and use it to buy one more stamp for my war savings certificate. This certificate was a booklet that held sixteen stamps, for a total of four dollars — to be redeemed by the government sometime after the war for five dollars. Since this was done in class time I always felt pleasantly virtuous buying another stamp. I didn't think of this at the time, but I'm sure those children who couldn't ever bring a quarter must have felt bad — a quarter was a lot of money to most of us then.

Victory gardens were another part of the war effort. The government encouraged everyone to grow vegetables for themselves, so that the commercial farmers' produce could be used to feed the army. We didn't have a Victory garden ourselves, but the area around St. Catharines was then all farmland, and I earned my first wages weeding carrots for twenty-five cents an hour or picking strawberries for three cents a basket.

Thinking back now to my high school years, I realize that all our teachers were either women or much older men. At the time that made no impression on me; I suppose I thought teachers were all old, as were ministers and doctors and bus drivers and janitors. I remember feeling rather excited when the young woman who had been my grade seven teacher joined the WAACS, and I envied her the chance to see new worlds.

Though there was no television in homes, I did occasionally go to the movies. It cost twelve cents for the movie, eight cents for the bus both ways, which left five cents for a chocolate bar — and used up all my allowance. At the movies I was confronted with world news in pictures, since every feature film was preceded by a short newsreel from Pathe News, "The Eyes and Ears of the World." But after the newsreel there was always a cartoon — and I'm ashamed to say I paid much more attention to the cartoon than to the newsreel. Once, when I was quite young, I was taken to a war film that had a scene I can still see in my mind's eye — it showed sailors hanging on to the edge of a ship and being picked off by a sniper, dropping to sure death in the waves below. I was too innocent then to know that those sailors were simply actors who would all survive to go home after the shoot, and so I wept for them and had nightmares about them. Strange, isn't it, that my most heartfelt tears were for pretend casualties?

For the first years of the war our household was lucky. We had no family member involved in the war, and so those years seemed to me to be rather romantic, really. The magazines were full of stories about lovers parting on train station platforms, or being reunited on docksides, or sometimes never reunited. There were also hundreds of movies with the same kinds of scenes. And there were songs — how there were songs! I can still remember the words to many of them: "Don't Sit Under the Apple Tree with Anyone Else but Me," "When the Lights Go On Again All over the World," "As Time Goes By," "Give a Cheer As You Wave Me Good-bye," "There'll Be Bluebirds over the White Cliffs of Dover." There was the "Boogie Woogie Woogie" by the

Andrews Sisters, which started the jitterbug craze.

And there were silly songs, too. I'm willing to bet that any adult over the age of sixty could still sing the whole of the nonsense song "Mairzy Doates."

I'm not sure just how I learned the words to these songs, for as I said there was only one radio in our house. (Even that small radio set was a marvel to us — we had none in our Mikage house, and used to go in to our Japanese neighbours' house on Christmas Day to listen to the King's Message on their shortwave radio.) Perhaps I learned some of them from records. Bob had entered one of those competitions that abounded in magazines ("Tell in 25 words or less why you like Colgate toothpaste best . . .") and to our amazement he won a wind-up record player. We had no records, mind you, but as he started working at summer jobs some of his money did go towards a few records, which he played endlessly. Many of his records were of trumpet music, since both he and my oldest brother, Hugh, played the trumpet. I sometimes think of my poor father, who was *not* musical, having to listen to Bob playing his trumpet in his bedroom, Hugh playing his in the basement, and me practising my scales on the piano in the living room, occasionally all at the same time . . .

As the war went on, my father worked away at his job, walking both ways every day — he had had bad experiences in the British Artillery in World War I and would never ride in a car or bus if he could help it. Nowadays I wonder: did he sit in that cramped office and dream of his classroom back in Osaka? Of his respectful students and the bowing villagers? Of the vast store of English poetry now trapped uselessly in his head? But back then I was filled with teenage concerns, and I never asked. His job was with the Wartime Housing Corporation, a government outfit that was putting up small prefabricated houses, temporary housing for those men who came to work at the factories in St. Catharines, all now making war supplies. He would be amused, I think, to know that much of that "temporary housing" is still being lived in today.

If my mother worried about the fate of Auntie 'No in those years she didn't say so to me — and in the throes of becoming a teenager I soon forgot my kindly Japanese "grandmother." I've sometimes wondered how I managed to wander through those years so blinkered against all the horrors. But recently I read a book about the 1940s in the United States which spoke of all teenagers then being "massively unconcerned with world problems." That made me feel that I wasn't alone in my blinkered state. And the only girls' magazine in those days, *Calling All Girls,* certainly had little in it about the war, just articles about fashions and hair styles and how to talk to boys.

A few things did pierce my self-centredness, like a poster for war bonds, which had a picture of a small child kneeling by her bed in a bombed-out London house. It seems that only make-believe things had the power to bring on my tears.

To be fair, while the war was on, ordinary people in North America knew nothing about forced labour camps or concentration camps or Prisoner of War camps. And perhaps the fact that there was no television then made it easier for teenagers to ignore what was going on. Today, with the television set dominating the living room or family room, the news broadcasts bring the fighting of any war right into our midst. One small radio tucked away in the den was much less intrusive.

For my mother, there had never been anything remotely romantic about these war years. With a son of my own now, I can easily imagine her fears and sleepless nights as my brother Hugh got closer and closer to the draft age. Around the time that he was in his last year of high school, the government introduced a scheme whereby young men of draft age could join the army and spend the first year at the University of Toronto, all expenses covered. This was a boon indeed, since at that time there was no university in St. Catharines, and the expense of university was daunting. So off Hugh went for a year of science studies, and my mother could relax. But after that came a year of drill in the infantry, preparatory to going overseas to fight. And my memories of the war might have been much sharper and sadder, for he was within a week of being shipped overseas when the cumbersome machinery of bureaucracy read his admission papers more carefully and noticed that he had once spoken Japanese fluently. Instead of overseas he went off to Vancouver, to study at the Japanese Language School there.

That brought another reprieve. And to a teenage girl, having a brother in a handsome lieutenant's uniform was quite dashing. From the Japanese Language School Hugh went into the Intelligence Service. Again, I can remember my mother's tears when I asked her, "But what does somebody in the Intelligence Service *do*?"

To which she answered, in a voice scarcely above a whisper, "Well, sometimes they become spies . . ."

But that was not to be Hugh's fate; he spent the rest of the war safely in Washington, seconded to the American Intelligence Service.

By the spring of 1945 the war in Europe was drawing to a close. I have a sharp memory of a girl standing by my locker at school, crying bitterly over the death of Roosevelt. And then it was VE Day — which was marred in St. Catharines by the death of a teenager in the celebrating crowds at Montebello Park. The momentous day of August 6, the beginning of the atomic age, is a hazier memory. No one at the time realized the enormous significance of that day for all the world. It ended the war; that was all that was important then.

Much, much later, we received a letter from Japan telling us that Auntie 'No had died very shortly after Pearl Harbor. I think my mother was glad she had been spared the griefs of war. Apart from that I was unusually lucky — the tragedies of war didn't touch our family. Not like my husband, an Englishman and not normally emotional, who never failed to observe Remembrance Day, weeping openly. My understanding of what the war had meant for others came much later, again through books and films: *Mrs. Miniver, The Diary of Anne Frank, Three Came Back,* and many, many others.

And yet . . . though Hugh returned safely, I think there was a casualty of the war in our family: my father. As I play my "What if" game again, I ask, "What if he hadn't died so soon after the war's end? What if he had been able to return to Japan?" He could have been so useful then, helping the Japanese people and the occupation forces understand each other, so busy and fulfilled. But he never saw again the country he had lived in for almost thirty years.

Nor did my mother, who died a year after he did. I was the only one of my family who felt that I just *had* to get back somehow. I went to the Canadian Academy in Kobe, becoming a teacher in the same grade two that I'd left eighteen years earlier. It was not the same classroom that I went back to, though. The Canadian Academy I had known was just a pile of rubble by this time. The only thing left for me to recognize was the swing, a big log suspended on chains, that we younger children had played on at recess times. Now the school had moved farther up the mountain to a new building. The school bell was an old air raid siren, and I used to worry that its wailing, four times a day, must surely bring back nightmare memories to the Japanese families down the hill.

I had been back in Japan about a month when I steeled myself one day to take the train from Kobe out to our village of Mikage. There had been much bomb damage there, too, and when I stepped off the train nothing looked familiar. But I vaguely remembered that we used to turn right from the train station to reach our house, so I set off in that direction. I wandered about the narrow streets for quite a while, recognizing nothing.

Then I turned a corner — and suddenly, there was our street: the Uenoyama of my childhood. The houses had all been destroyed and rebuilt; none of them looked familiar. But the street itself, of ridged concrete, bounded by low stone walls — it was still there.

And in that moment I felt as if I had travelled back in time. I felt that I was seven years old again . . . and if I put my hand up I would feel my father's hand there, waiting for mine.

Then I turned a corner — and suddenly there was our street. In that moment I felt as if I had travelled back in time.

DOROTHY JOAN HARRIS *studied languages at university, taught for a year in France, and managed to fulfill her dream of returning to Japan by applying to teach at her old school in Kobe. The teaching contract was for three years, but with very poor timing, she became engaged the night before leaving for Japan (to an Englishman she had met in a British youth hostel) so she returned to Canada after one year away. She was an editor in Toronto for several years, still fascinated by books, still wanting to write "when she had the time." But it was when she was at home with her two small children, and had no free time at all, that she began to write: stories for and about her children. These stories have grown into fifteen books for children: picture books, easy readers, and Young Adult novels.*

ROCH CARRIER

translated from the French by Sheila Fischman

I was eight years old on August 6, 1945, when the explosion of an atom bomb wiped out the city of Hiroshima, in Japan.

Men, women, and children perished: more than 100,000 of them. I have no memory of that day. How is it possible? Never before in all of known history has mankind's destructive genius manifested itself in such dazzling fashion. I don't remember.

Eight-year-olds are easily astonished. I must have been struck by the power of the bomb. I don't remember. It was the end of summer holidays. Soon we would be going back to school. Had I on that day gone with my two friends on an expedition into the forest that circled our village? Had we taken off on one of our frequent forays into space like Buck Rogers? With our capes on our backs, were we busy flying like Superman above the church steeple?

I do not remember the tragic explosion at Hiroshima. Yet I'm certain that our parents talked again and again about the bomb that had made the earth tremble when it burst. I'm sure that they fretted: Was this the beginning of the end of the world?

Of those days of terror I can recall just one incident. It happened a few days later. At the garage where my father had his black Ford repaired, the insurance salesman was describing to a fat farmer the gigantic explosion of the atomic bomb.

"It was so powerful," he said, "if it had happened at the other end of Canada, in the water of the Pacific Ocean, people here in Québec would have got splashed. There would've been so much water in our village that even in the church on the hill, the Curé would have had to put his boots on to say Mass."

It's frustrating not being able to find in my cluttered memory a single recollection of the Hiroshima disaster. A whole city was destroyed in less than one second. It was the biggest massacre that ever happened. I had never even seen anything like it in the comic strips. How can I not remember that day? It was the day of the Great Barbarity. Man's wickedness was displacing that of Satan. On that day, Satan became nothing more than some quaint and picturesque character.

In contrast, when war was declared on September 3, 1939, when I was two years old, I can evoke that day very clearly. I was sitting in my high chair. My father was feeding me little pieces of pancake rolled in brown sugar and maple syrup from the tip of his fork. I was wolfing it down and I was happy. Suddenly the door was flung open and my uncle appeared, wearing a long black robe and opening a newspaper. "It's war!" he announced.

Now, nearly sixty years later, I have not forgotten. My uncle was pale. Was it his fear that impressed me? Did my father react with words of fear? Did he stop stuffing me with pancakes? Was my mother worried about what would happen to our father, to our house, if there was a war? She remembered how preoccupied her own mother had been during World War I. I in my high chair knew nothing about that; I didn't know yet how much mothers worry, but on that morning something happened. What was it? I don't know. I was two years old and I wanted nothing more than a pancake with brown sugar and maple syrup. But on that morning I sensed that life was changing. That nothing was as it had been before.

Am I fantasizing? You don't believe that a child of two can recall for the rest of his life a certain morning in September? I didn't believe it either. I talked about it with my uncle, who is old now. His memory did not record that particular morning when he delivered us the bad news in the newspaper. At the time he was studying to become a priest. He was obliged to wear a long black soutane. It got in his way when he played tennis or baseball. Every morning, he went up to the church to recite his prayers, the prayers of a future priest, and on his way down he brought my parents the newspaper. And so it's possible that my memory is correct.

I was very young. After that day my parents often disappeared behind the newspaper. They would emerge from it filled with consternation, just like they were when there was a death in the village. I didn't understand. My parents were worried. They were afraid. They feared the days to come. They read parts of the newspaper to one another. How could I have understood? They were saying words I'd never heard before, words that weren't familiar even to them. Their voices then were not their usual voices. When they carried me up to bed I didn't fall asleep, because of the monster hiding in the night, outside the window. I could hear it brush against the walls of the house.

At news time, my father brought his ear close to the radio to hear it better. We had to be silent then. I wasn't even allowed to cry. I always did my best to cry during the news. I hated being neglected. Instead of picking me up in her arms, my mother would lose patience and make more noise than I did. A few times she spanked me for abusing my freedom of expression. She wasn't the same person.

While the news was on, my brothers and I were forbidden to have fun.

Yet that was when we had the most fun.

The radio crackled like an egg that's cooking in the frying pan. Since we were forced to be silent, I would come close to my father and try to listen the way he did. The story the radio was telling was long and involved. I wasn't even very interested, though I could tell that what was happening was important.

I was more curious to spy on what was going on inside the radio. I would slip in behind and, closing one eye like someone who's looking through a keyhole, I observed. The tubes looked like little men with an electric spark for a smile. Which of the little men was recounting the bad news from the war?

That was how I found out that in a war, soldiers killed other soldiers. Cannons set fire to houses. They burst into flames like barns in the country when lightning strikes. All these miseries were going on far, far away, in the Old Countries.

Often when they were talking about the calamities of war, our parents whispered. They didn't want those horrors to give us nightmares. Did they think that we'd be better protected from the calamities if they talked about them only in a murmur? Did they want to keep us children from knowing how cruel adults can become? Or did they just want to protect our childhood and let us believe in the beauty of the world?

Soon I was big enough to go sliding with my older brother in his sleigh. He didn't like playing with a baby but he had to take me, our mother made him. And so we'd climb the hill. From the summit, near the church, I could see other hills and, behind them, other hills even farther away. How far we could see! My brother assured me that even farther away were the Old Countries and the war.

I turned my gaze all the way to the horizon and I could make out images I'd seen in the newspaper: soldiers covered with blood like deer during hunting season; houses crumbled by fires; children frightened because they had no parents; parents who had lost their children; women, men, children with nothing to eat; many dead bodies lying in the street.

The war was still far away. When it came to my village I would escape with my big brother on his sleigh. But how would my father, my mother, and my little brother run away? I was worried and that was what I thought about before I fell asleep.

Here, under a cottony sky, the winter was peaceful. From the chimneys of all our houses warm smoke rose into the sky. The sunny silence glittered on the snow. There were no children who were too thin because they were starving. No booming cannons. The church and all the houses were standing. The only racket was caused by the squawking of children at play and the cheeping of birds. At the sawmill, too, the teeth of the circular saw creaked in the pine logs. I shouldn't have felt sad because of the war.

In my brother's sleigh at the top of our hill, I was thinking, as our parents said, that God was very good because He hadn't sent the war to our village. I looked up at the blue sky where He lived, I looked at the clouds where His angels resided, I looked at the steeple of the church that was His house in our village, and I loved Him very much. But I wished I could understand why He had allowed war to rage in the Old Countries.

From his meetings at the general store or his travels through the neighbouring countryside, our father brought home the news. One day he came home with the story that there had been German soldiers in the great River that runs through the Gaspé. They had got out of their submarine. And they'd been spotted on the shores of certain villages. Apparently they were trying to buy food. If the war came to our country, our anguish would be like the anguish in the Old Countries.

Later I realized that even French-Canadian soldiers had been killed in the war. I didn't know the meaning of the words "French Canadian," but I noticed that whenever a French-Canadian soldier lost his life, my parents looked as sad as if he'd been a member of our family.

I looked over my father's shoulder at a photograph of soldiers who'd been killed in the war. I peered at their faces. I didn't understand. They were dead but they were smiling as if they were happy. I had seen some dead people in their coffins. They weren't smiling. They didn't look as if they were happy to be dead. I didn't understand the soldiers' smiles. When you're five years old, the world is very complicated.

What shyness kept me from asking my parents to explain this mystery? I had heard them whispering that in many cases, the dead soldiers' bodies hadn't been found. What did that mean? If their bodies hadn't been found, how could they be smiling in the newspaper? When she took out her Kodak, our mother (who only wanted to take happy photos) would say: "Smile!" Was there someone in the war who said "Smile!" to the soldiers? I was so absorbed by these mysteries! But in this complicated world I got used to not getting an answer to my questions.

Our parents often whispered on the sly. So many things that weren't supposed to be heard by us, the children. But we did our best to catch them out in their secrets. And then we'd exchange our bits of stories.

That was how we learned about a man who had refused to go and fight in the war. The army police had come to pick him up. According to our parents' whispers, the deserter had hidden out in the forest. The police, they thought, hadn't dared to venture into the deep snow. Another deserter had hidden in a barn, under the hay. The police came back. They poked around in the hay with pitchforks. The pitchfork's teeth, which were pointed like swords, sank in right beside the deserter's head. He stayed there, as motionless as a dead man. In their stories the deserter was never flushed out, and the police always left our village empty-handed.

One night, a man was walking down the street, his head down but his eyes constantly assessing the situation first on his left, then on his right. We were out on the verandah. He looked very strange. In an undertone, our mother explained that ever since he'd been a deserter, the man didn't trust anyone. I liked these stories about men who defied the police. I thought they were brave. When the army police came to get me, I would become a deserter like them. I admired those men who refused to go to the Old Countries and get killed. I felt a natural sympathy for them. I guessed that these men were terrified of the war. As I was. Perhaps I liked them because I shared their fear.

One winter day our village was shattered by a military funeral. Was I taken to the church for this very unusual event? Or did I just see the cortège wend its way down the snow-covered street? This funeral was unlike the funerals of the old people who died now and then. This was the solemn burial of a soldier. I still had never seen a soldier, either alive or dead. That day the soldiers weren't in the Old Countries but in our own village, wearing long khaki coats with golden buttons. On their shoulders they were carrying a coffin and inside it lay the dead soldier, whom we couldn't see. Ahead of the coffin was another soldier who was holding a bugle. For a long time I was obsessed by that scene. I often saw it again before I went to sleep in my little bed.

Because of the war, the government asked us to save on everything. For instance, we just turned on one light at a time and we just lit one room in the house. We went to bed early so we'd use less electricity. The factories needed it for making weapons. Without weapons it was impossible to destroy the enemies: that was what our parents explained to us. Meat, sugar, even tea were rationed. Otherwise the soldiers who were at war in the Old Countries wouldn't have enough to eat. In the Old Countries there was nothing to eat. We also had to save on gasoline. Our father stopped our Sunday drives in his bright and shiny black Ford. He didn't mind too much. Now after a long week he could finally take a nap on Sunday. Thanks to the gasoline our father saved, the planes and tanks could defeat the enemies. The longer our father napped, the more gasoline he was saving and the more enemies would be killed. As our father snored, I could sense that victory was near.

To control the consumption of gasoline, sugar, butter, meat, and flour, the government issued coupons to present to the merchants. Without coupons it was impossible to buy those goods. That was rationing. Everyone complained about it. When our father came home, his shirt pocket was bulging with coupons. We couldn't afford to buy everything we were entitled to. I was proud to have a father who accumulated more coupons than all the other fathers.

My admiration would grow even greater. The factories that made planes, tanks, boats, jeeps, and cannons needed metal. It said so in the newspaper. Our father couldn't be indifferent. He began to collect from the farmers scrap iron, pipes, old nails, chunks of the skeletons of old automobiles. Behind the house we soon had a patriotic heap of twisted and rusted scrap metal that threatened the carrots in our mother's Victory garden. We asked our friends over to look at it. I was overflowing with pride. With the metal our father collected they would be able to make lots of arms to kill lots of enemies. Standing on top of the pile I sensed that with our father, the Allies would triumph!

Even the Laura Secord Candy Company turned its production to tanks — albeit cardboard ones. This box had a lift-off turret and wheels for easy rolling. Imaginative packaging such as this was some compensation for the shortage of sweets available to us.

How innocent I was during this phase of perverse cruelty. But *were* we all that innocent? We had our own wars with our wooden rifles: "Bang! You're dead!" On the battlefield without cover, we were often hit. We'd fall to the ground. We had horrible convulsions. We would roll on the ground. We'd clutch our bellies ripped open by shrapnel. We'd get up only to crumple to the ground again. Then we would die, moaning. And when we'd finished dying, we would start another war.

Were we children all that innocent? We had our own wars with our wooden rifles. And while our entire generation of children was at play, we were given toys that encouraged us to . . .

bomb Berlin,

sink submarines,

blow apart and piece together,

punch Hitler with every step we took,

humiliate our enemies,

and dream of going off to war.

There were some who didn't want to die anymore. They complained. It wasn't fair: why did they have to die all the time while others never did? Why were others allowed to shout: "Bang! You're dead!" Why was it never their turn to kill? That right was only given to them after a skirmish, complete with scratched faces, bloody noses, skinned knees, buttons wrenched off, torn pants. Often, a spanking by our mothers would restore peace. We'd be exiled to our rooms.

There, in the silence, I would ask God to forgive me for fighting. I would have liked to ask Him for something else, too, but I didn't dare. If He was perfectly good, as the priest, the teacher, and our mother assured us He was, why had He sent the epidemic of war to the Old Countries?

One day, our father came home with a big poster rolled up under his arm. He hung it on the wall of the garage where he parked his Ford. It was his favourite room in the whole house. He was very fond of his car. The drawing on the poster terrorized me. Our friends could come to look at it as long as they didn't so much as brush against the Ford. They, too, were frozen by the horror on the poster.

During the war, posters portrayed Nazis as monsters, capable of cruelty beyond imagining.

Nazis, extremely big, wearing grey uniforms and very high caps decorated with black swastikas and armbands that also bore swastikas, were holding big black revolvers. The mouths of the revolvers were resting against the shaved heads of children our age who certainly hadn't eaten for a long time. The Nazis, who had broad shoulders and square chins, were smiling. They enjoyed frightening the children. Those Nazis gave me the shivers.

I clenched my little fists as I looked at those barbarians. I wished that I weren't a mere child. I wanted to be a man. I would take my hunting rifle and go to the war. I would fire a bullet into the hearts of those Nazis who terrorized children my age. Why were their heads shaved? Our father kept that poster on the wall long after the end of the war. It still scared us.

When peace was restored the soldiers came home. They paraded without their rifles, all of them marching in step, filling the entire width of the street. It was to impress the girls watching at their windows from behind the lace curtains. They wanted it known that they were soldiers. They wanted it known that they'd won the war. They wanted it known that they'd come back. Now there was peace but they still wore their soldiers' uniforms. They wore them even when they got together to drink beer. They drank so much that they had trouble walking down the street. And then they would sing. They sang very loud. Those who couldn't sing shouted words that insulted God.

Those soldiers had come back alive. They had killed enemies. My friends and I all agreed: the soldiers were bigger heroes than the deserters who had got away from the police. The deserters hadn't killed any enemies: zero enemies. Since the warriors' return, according to our parents' whispers, the deserters dared not show themselves in the daylight.

We children observed the soldiers without getting too close to them. Our parents didn't approve of their boasting. Also, they insinuated that the soldiers had "seen things" in the Old Countries. We children wondered what those things could be. The soldiers started wearing normal clothes. But over them they still wore their military tunics. What was it that they'd seen during the war?

Our parents grew impatient when I questioned them. They became mysterious when they talked about those things. What was it that the soldiers had seen in the Old Countries? All we could do was listen in on conversations. Very little did we understand.

First of all, the soldiers had seen the war. It was terrible and ugly. In their impenetrable stories, our parents told how before the battles, the soldiers consumed drugs to cure their fear and make them mean. Our parents knew all kinds of ugly things. They also knew that our soldiers had been poisoned by gases that the enemies sprayed onto the battlefields. Apparently those gases took away their enjoyment of life.

Besides, according to our parents, certain soldiers had done things with girls that aren't done in a Catholic country like Canada, but that are done a lot in pagan lands like the Old Countries. Our parents were scandalized. How could we children understand these complicated things?

We studied the soldiers, we were jealous of them because they had lived through adventures like the heroes in our comic strips. Our own lives were so restricted. The soldiers were coming back from so far away. One day I, too, would travel far, like them.

Did I dream then about piloting airplanes, about bombing enemy cities, about infiltrating behind enemy lines, about flinging a grenade into a trench, about getting hold of a machine gun? I don't remember. However, I've forgotten nothing about how I tried with my two best friends to fly like Superman. I would hurl myself off a beam in the barn and land in the hay.

That time was not an ordinary time. Not only was there a war on but some women in the village dared to smoke like men. Husbands complained about finding cigarette ashes in the bread their wives kneaded. There were even some women who were no longer afraid to drive a car. They would fly down the street blowing their horn, one elbow resting on the window just like a real man. "What is this world coming to?" my mother would sigh.

What have I retained from this period of my life? First of all, I have the unshakeable certainty that in a privileged country I was a privileged child. Elsewhere in the world thousands of children like me, children my own age, were condemned to hell on earth. And while they were suffering the torments of the war, I was living in a village where the only noise was the sound that was sometimes made by my sleigh gliding over the snow. I have always felt, and I still feel, that I owe a debt to those children.

Children have the fundamental right to live at peace. Why were those children of my own childhood condemned by adults to war? By what right? For what sin were they given such a punishment? No theory, no philosophy, no religion has ever been able to explain that injustice.

From that childhood experience I have kept another certainty: nothing, absolutely nothing, can justify the horrors of war. Its devastating effects are disproportionate to its cause. Winners and losers are both guilty of allowing themselves to be dragged into raving madness. No problem is so insoluble that humans must be killed to settle it.

Later on, I read a great deal to try to understand this worldwide conflict. Historians explained its causes, its origins. But I closed my books perplexed: How could so many lives be broken off, so many towns destroyed, so much suffering imposed, so much future wiped out — for that?

What would have become of those millions of victims if they hadn't been sentenced to death? No imagination is powerful enough to conceive of what the present time would be like if the victims of war weren't absent. What a waste! I think about the children who weren't born, about those who didn't grow up, about all the young men and young women who were done away with. So many dreams, so much talent was murdered. War ravages the future even more than the present. What a tremendous waste! The leader who starts a war must have very little regard for those who come after him.

From that comes a moral obligation. Certain countries (thanks to the wisdom of their citizens and their leaders, or pure chance) enjoy the privilege of peace. It is the duty of those countries to relieve the suffering of others who are at war. The citizens of our peaceful Canada do not have the right to live with no concern for the misery of others. That is why we must, for instance, support Canada's efforts in peace initiatives in zones that are poisoned by violence. This mission is not as easy as sitting down to write in a newspaper that the initiative hasn't been properly carried out.

Remembering the deserters of my childhood helps me to understand that in the face of war, fear can become too terrifying and intolerable, anguish can become too heavy, sorrow too intense.

It is normal that victims should aspire to leave hell behind and become part of human brotherhood again beneath a sky that reminds us of a great truth: All humans are travelling in the same ship, which is called Earth. When we pass through storms the entire vessel is shaken. All of us then share a responsibility: to survive the storm. Whatever our beliefs, our heritage, our history, our colour, our differences, we have all of us come from the unknown and we are all heading back to it. The little time we possess during our lives shouldn't be squandered by squabbles on board. All of us are born in the same way and similarly all of us are doomed to die.

War is a punishment that adults, in a moment of atavistic madness, inflict on children. When adults truly love children (and old people, who are like aged children) they do not make war. That conviction, too, is deeply rooted in my childhood. Of course, we in my village couldn't hear the booming cannons of war. But they were behind the hills, on the other side of the ocean, and I listened to their silence. All that I saw around me was the peace.

I worried a lot about the inhabitants of the Old Countries. From that perhaps comes the curiosity, the sympathy, the affection I have for many countries on our planet. I have travelled in order to discover them, to understand them, to forge friendships, to share the peace I have inherited.

The more we explore life, the more we discover that events are woven in an astonishing fashion. The knots that tie them together are marvels of unforeseeable invention. A single life harbours more of the unknown than the most unknown of the planets. To live a life is the most incredible adventure.

Far from the war, these are some of the certainties that I gathered in the peace of my village for the time when I would become a man.

ROCH CARRIER *has succeeded brilliantly in many different ways. A novelist and dramatist, he has written stage adaptations of two of his novels, one for the Stratford Festival and one for the National Arts Centre in Ottawa. He has been Director of the Canada Council (his term ended in 1997) and is an Officer of the Order of Canada. A Québec Liberal, Roch has thrown himself with increasing passion into the cause of keeping a strong Québec in Canada. He and his companion Nina share four children and two (soon to be three) grandchildren; other children love him especially as the man who wrote* The Hockey Sweater. *Carrier grew up in a small village — he still likes to use rural communities as settings for his literary work; he also enjoys exotic travel, most recently in Africa.*

JEAN LITTLE

I sat in Loews Theatre staring at the movie screen.

I had both hands pressed tightly over my ears, and I kept shutting my eyes and then opening them a slit only to squeeze them shut again.

In *Son of Lassie*, the wounded serviceman and his gallant dog were hiding from a troop of Germans who were hunting them down with intent to kill. Any second, I was convinced, dog and man were going to be caught, tortured, and executed before my very eyes. I could not bear it.

If my mother had been there, she would have put her arm around me and murmured, "It's only a story, Jean. Everything will be all right in the end. It's only a story."

But I was visiting my cousin and her mother in Toronto. Mother was sixty miles away in Guelph. Dorothy, a well-behaved, only child a year younger than I, was much too young to serve as my shield and buckler.

Suddenly one of the Germans raised his rifle and fired. With a spring, I was out of my front-row seat and under the stage, crouching among a litter of candy wrappers. Now, with both eyes and ears as closed as I could get them, I was moaning, "Tell me when it's over. Tell me when it's over."

Dorothy, shocked and mortified, tried to haul me forth.

"Come OUT!" she entreated. "Please, Jean, come out now."

I uncovered half an ear and listened. No shooting. The music had calmed down. I inched forward and twisted my head to peer up at the cliff-like screen. The bad part was over. I wriggled up onto my seat again, grinning sheepishly.

"Really," muttered my poor cousin, "it's only a story."

But it had not seemed only a story to me. Although I knew that I was safe enough in Loews Theatre, I also knew that it was wartime not only in the film but in the world. War was terrifying. Children even younger than I huddled in air raid shelters listening to bombs falling. Sometimes babies got killed as well as dogs like Lassie.

My first real brush with war had come when I was five. A bomber, returning to its base, unloaded a stick of bombs over the paddy fields directly behind our home in Taiwan. We heard the drone of a low-flying airplane and rushed outside to stare up at it. I had never seen a plane before. I had been born blind and, although I now could see, I was still "legally blind." I had to be twenty feet away from something to see details that people with normal vision saw clearly from a distance of two hundred feet. I could see trees, for instance, but not individual leaves. I could see stars but never more than a dozen. Planes had been invisible until this day, partly because they flew too high for my limited vision to spot them and partly because, in 1937, they were still rare. I did see this one, however. As I gazed up at it, wondering if it was even going to clear the roof, the bombs smashed into the rice field. There was so much noise that I could not hear myself screaming. The solid, hitherto immovable ground under my feet bucked and shook as though it were alive.

My brothers, Jamie and Hugh, and I turned as one to run to inspect the damage, but my father's voice stopped us in our tracks.

"Stay where you are," he thundered. "Not one of you is to go back there. There may be an unexploded bomb waiting for you to detonate it. It could blow you to smithereens."

When my father, Llew Little, spoke in that voice, nobody argued. I was sufficiently scared to spend most of the day safely indoors but the boys were outraged. Their Taiwanese friends had gone running back there the moment the earth stood still. It wasn't fair.

Other than teaching me that dropped bombs can make the earth quake and leave gaping craters in the ground, this incident changed nothing in my young life. Although I was aware of my father's tension, I did not guess he was afraid. In bed that night, I pondered deliciously on what would have happened to us if we had been in the paddy field when the bombs hit. Yet the terrifying prospect had no reality for me. I had never encountered violent death outside a book, and I believed myself and my immediate family to be immortal.

Early in 1939, my missionary family moved to Hong Kong. I went to school for the first time, and my teacher advised my parents to take me to Canada and enroll me in a "Sight Saving Class," a new program for children with poor vision. My father was convinced we were on the brink of war. The teacher's suggestion gave him his excuse. He bought our steamship tickets that very day. My mother thought his fears were groundless but if we had remained in Hong Kong, we would have been interned as prisoners of war when Japan invaded Hong Kong only a few months later.

Dad himself could not come with us since he had agreed to take another doctor's place in a hospital in Kobe, Japan, for a year, but Mother and we four children set sail for Canada in the summer of 1939.

As we prepared to embark, talk of war was everywhere. I kept hearing two words: submarine and torpedo. My brother Jamie terrified me by explaining the meaning of each in garish detail.

"Don't tell Mother," he said. "It might worry her."

I did not tell but she must have guessed from my nightmares.

Lifeboat drills also frightened me. When the whistle went, we were to race to our station where Mother would meet us. Then the family was to stand, hugging lifebelts, ready to jump down into a lifeboat far below. Although I was secretly convinced I would be unable to jump if worst came to worst, my real terror was that I would not be able to find my mother in all the pushing throng. After all, we were not with her every minute. We had a whole great ship as our playground. But after the first drill, whenever I remembered, I tried hard not to let her out of my sight just in case. This meant missing some fun with my brothers, but how appalling if I were to find myself bobbing around the Pacific Ocean in the wrong lifeboat!

We were safely in Toronto in September, however, when war was declared. I was only seven and I do not remember anything about that morning. When Christmas neared, we got up one day before sunrise to go to Union Station to meet Dad, who was visiting us for Christmas. I had not seen him for over six months and I was afraid I might not know him. My baby sister, Pat, who was just one and a half, only knew him because the boys and I had kept showing her his photograph and telling her to say "Daddy." I was holding onto her when he came through the crowd of people at the gate. Pat was slow at talking, but when he took her in his arms, she reached up, patted his bristly cheek, and murmured "Daddy." Jamie, Hugh, and I grinned at each other.

For this family portrait with Grandma and Mother, Jamie, Hugh, Pat, and I were on our best behaviour. After we moved to Guelph, we became known as "those wild children of Dr. Little's."

We listened to Princess Elizabeth and Princess Margaret Rose send us greetings over the radio waves that Christmas. Although Canadians had not begun to leave for the front yet, I heard enough about what was happening in Europe to decide that people who fought wars against other people were stupid.

"If I were made Queen of the world," I told my father that Christmas, "I'd make it against the law to go to war."

It seemed an obvious solution but Dad was not thunderstruck by my brilliance.

"You have something there," he said, only half-listening.

Disappointed by this, I told Mother. She sighed.

"I was so sure we'd never go to war again," she said, her voice troubled. "But Llew was right. He told me last night that people in Hong Kong are all but climbing the walls trying to get passage out before the Japanese arrive."

Later I learned that her big brother Gordon had been killed in World War I. His plane had exploded over England as a result of sabotage. I gazed at his picture. He looked special and remote and heroic. He did not look real to me.

Most of the war was like that. We played games in which the bad guys were Germans and the good guys Canadians. When we went to the movies, we saw black-and-white newsreels showing Nazi soldiers goose-stepping down foreign streets. We laughed at them and imitated their ridiculous strutting at home. We said "Heil Hitler" and saluted like the Gestapo. It was part of the "war" game.

I still know the songs we learned during those years: "There'll Always Be an England," "Til the Lights of London Shine Again," and "There'll Be Bluebirds over the White Cliffs of Dover." And we sang ditties in the playground:

"Whistle while you work,
Mussolini bought a shirt.
Hitler wore it. Britain tore it.
Whistle while you work."

The moment Dad completed his year in Kobe, he came to Toronto and announced that we were moving to his hometown of Guelph. We went late in November during a howling blizzard. He and Mother set up a joint medical practice. He thought perhaps a few women and children might come to the only woman doctor in town, but, at first, her job was that of "a glorified office nurse." Dad was regarded as the real doctor by most of the patients.

For months, he tried to enlist but was turned down. After all, he was forty-two and he had a wife and four children.

I was in grade four now. I was a social misfit. I had crossed eyes, poor vision, told lies, tattled on other children, and cried when I was teased. I still was not sure how Canadians behaved either. I did not fully understand such customs as going out on Halloween or setting off firecrackers on the twenty-fourth of May. Looking back, I believe my year in fourth grade was perhaps the unhappiest year of my life.

That winter, Aunt Eva came to visit and told us about a trick played on her by her paper boy.

"Give me a nickel and I'll snow you a trick," he had said.

When she gave him the coin, he shoved a bit of folded paper into her hand, and took off. It said:

"This nickel goes to a fund to help purchase a donkey to
Kick Hitler out of Germany. Don't be an ass and whine.
Get your nickel back the way I got mine."

I copied out this hilarious missive and took the paper to school. When I showed it to the other girls in the cloakroom, they said in sneering voices, "Dare you to do it to Mr. Johnson."

I was usually a great coward but I knew Mr. Johnson liked me and I decided to show them I was not the weakling they imagined. Chin in the air, knees trembling, I marched up to his desk and said, "Mr. Johnson, give me a nickel and I'll show you a trick."

He looked down at me quizzically. Then he handed over a nickel. I dropped my paper, scrunched up and damp with sweat, on the desktop and scuttled to my desk. What would he do? Was I in for BIG trouble?

Mr. Johnson flicked the paper open and glanced at the pencilled words. Then, without a word to my quavering self, he shoved the page into his pocket and called the class to order. All day I waited for him to pounce but he said nothing about my trick. And I had a nickel, which, in those faraway days, had buying power. I breathed a sigh of relief and began to plan how to spend my small fortune.

Then Mr. Johnson came to our house for supper. I was pleased to see him. I had on my gypsy dress with the laced-up bodice and the flowered skirt and sleeves. Feeling special and proud, I bowed my head for the blessing and then picked up my fork. Before I could take in my first bite, I heard my teacher say to my father, "Dr. Little, give me a nickel and I'll show you a trick."

I leapt up and prepared to make a run for it, but Mother caught hold of my wrist.

"Sit down, Jean," she said quietly.

I do not remember what happened when my father read the note I had written about purchasing that donkey. My suspicion now is that it was a little lesson arranged for me by my teacher and my parents. I learned, from the experience, that it isn't doing wrong that bothers a person but it is being caught at it. I did not waste a thought on that fund to "kick Hitler out of

Germany." Hitler was the arch villain in all our games but, for us, he was like the evil forces in our comic books, not a person we personally feared.

I do not think it ever once crossed my mind nor the minds of my schoolfellows that Hitler might win the war and we would be punished for fighting against the Germans. We had all heard Winston Churchill's words about how we would fight until we won. His deep, rumbling voice was utterly convincing.

When I remember those years, I remember the books I read; the games I played with my small sister, Pat; going out on Halloween; the little books of Famous Players movie tickets Uncle Bill gave us each Christmas; our dog, Chum; the first poem I ever wrote; trying to be a good sport when I lost at Parcheesi. I remember many moments, some whole scenes, but hardly any of them reflect the fact that my country was fighting a world war. It was not only that I was too young to fight; it was that the fighting was far away.

At the end of 1940, the war intensified and, hearing that the navy had need of doctors, Dad tried enlisting yet again and was made a Lieutenant Commander. He went off to Esquimalt to be trained and then came home for a last leave before sailing for Britain.

There were buzz bombs over England. Would one of them kill my father? I tried to imagine this but could not. I secretly believed he would remain indomitable and face down any bomb, any bullet, any advancing tank, any sneaky torpedo.

Jamie was sent to St. Andrew's College. Dad did not think life in a houseful of women was good for a boy who was beginning high school. Pat, age three, stayed home with Grandma when Mother, Hugh, and I took my father to the train station when his leave ended. We were excited, chasing each other around on the platform, only rushing back to wave at the last minute. But, when we were driving home without him, we realized that Mother was in tears. She cried over sad books and movies but never just driving along in the car. We were both shocked. Hugh was also bewildered.

"Mummy, why are you crying?" he asked, staring at her.

I poked him hard and glared him into silence. But I was as disturbed as he. Mother was the strongest person we knew. Were we in danger? Was she afraid? She did not answer Hugh. I was scared to put his question again.

A few months later, when I had turned ten, I stood and watched troops marching down a Guelph street behind a band. They were off to war and yet they sang: no cares had they to grieve them, no pretty little girls to deceive them . . .

They sounded happy as larks, and the stirring band music added to the jaunty mood. I tried to force myself to picture them coming home with no arms or on crutches or too shell-shocked to live normal lives but I couldn't. The band music made me want to march away in their train. If only I knew how to get back in step. That was what really mattered, staying in step. Then they were gone and I walked on home, feeling confused. Was war the music or the wounds?

We bought war saving stamps with our allowance. We were supposed to get our money back once the war was over. By the time I remembered, my father had already cashed them in and, without consulting me, spent my fortune on a serviceable winter coat for me. I thought this highly unethical but knew better than to argue.

We collected milkweed pods to be made into parachutes. This sounded like balderdash to me but I still looked for them. We collected tin cans and any other junk metal. We had ration books. We planted Victory gardens. Ours was a disaster. We had not one green thumb among us.

Early in the war years, British children were sent to Canada to keep them safe from the frequent bombing raids punishing England. We called such boys and girls "War Guests." I would stare sideways at Shirley Russel, the evacuee in my class, and wonder how she could look so self-possessed and confident when her parents were so far away and in such peril. Shirley and her brother Ian did live with an aunt and uncle but I couldn't imagine living

British children were sent to Canada to keep them safe from the bombs falling on England. We called such boys and girls "War Guests." I couldn't imagine living separated from my mother.

separated from my mother. I began to think like a writer as I wondered what was going on behind Shirley's pretty face.

The one deprivation I really resented most bitterly was not getting a rubber doll like my cousin Dorothy's. Plastic had not yet been invented and rubber came from rubber trees in war-torn parts of the world like Malaya. Dorothy could bathe her doll. Mine had to be kept dry if they were to survive.

My father's being overseas for a big chunk of my childhood was, of course, a much worse deprivation than not having a rubber doll like Dorothy's. But I took his absence more or less for granted. Our house was full of people, we four children, our grandmother, Mother, often Aunt Gretta and a girl or woman who lived with us and helped Grandma run the house. It did not trouble me that, except for my younger brother, my family was entirely female. I did not wonder how this dearth of men I could respect and love would contribute to my sense of inadequacy when, as a teenager, I was supposed to chat to and charm adolescent boys. I might have been uncomfortable around them in any case, but my father's being away in the navy and Jamie's being packed off to boarding school kept me from learning how to make friends with boys. Hugh, after all, was two years younger and so did not count.

We wrote Dad letters while he was away, drew him pictures, had our pictures taken to send to him. He mailed home pictures of himself too, funny ones of him wearing a scruffy beard and smoking a pipe.

Instead of my father asking the blessing, we began to sing it. Mother gave us our allowances. She also grew much busier in the office. With many of the Guelph doctors away, those still there were overworked. We went unsupervised and became known as "those wild children of Dr. Little's." My Grandma lectured us constantly about being good examples but when we complained to Mother, she said we were just fine.

The war in Europe ended when I was in grade eight. We knew the end was near so, when the sirens began to blow, we started cheering. Mr. Benham said, "Stay right where you are while I check."

Two minutes later he came back, his face one big grin, and, throwing up his hands, cried, "The war is over. You can all go home for the rest of the day!"

What wild excitement as we piled out of that school building! For once, I was not the one handicapped kid, the lonely outsider, but one of the screeching mob, rushing out into the May sunshine, free from school, free from Hitler.

VJ Day passed almost unnoticed since I was at camp. I don't remember anything about the atom bombs being dropped until I saw the pictures of the mushroom cloud in *Life* magazine. Even then, we did not guess at the long-lasting horrors inflicted on the people in Nagasaki and Hiroshima. It took time for the truth to be revealed just as it took time for us to realize what had happened in Auschwitz and Bergen Belsen.

Then, one by one over the next months, the servicemen came home. How strange it was when Dad came home, first on leave and then when the war ended. All of a sudden, he was the one who gave us our allowances and we had to ask his permission to do things instead of only Mother's. We were not sure how to treat him. We could not read his moods. We were in awe of him during the first months and we went on turning to Mother as a matter of course. Tension blew up at unexpected moments and we were not sure what we had done to set it off. He had gone away a healthy man just entering middle age; he returned with diabetes and a heart condition and his youth gone. He was too arthritic to shake down a thermometer. And Mother was no longer willing to be his assistant. She had kept the practice going during his absence and had acquired new patients about whom he knew nothing. None of this was discussed with us openly but we all felt the charged atmosphere as the two of them worked to sort out their new roles as parents and doctors.

Some of my high school teachers were veterans struggling to fit into a world at peace. They returned from overseas as I and my peers entered high school with its unsettling challenges. We watched them and were sometimes puzzled by their restlessness, their inattention, and their abrupt mood swings.

Portrait of my father in 1945 by Evan Macdonald. Dad had been made a Lieutenant Commander in 1940.

We were too young to think of teachers as human beings like ourselves, but every so often, we were reminded that their world was as filled with unexpected demands as our own. The following year, I, for one, no longer speculated about their private lives. Later I was taught by a man who had been blinded during the war. He was taciturn, bitter, and cut adrift. Because of my own visual handicap, he frightened me. I never saw him when he was not surly. Had it been the war that had robbed him of courtesy, not to mention joy, or had he always been angry at life? Years later, when I lost most of my limited vision, I thought of him often and struggled to control my own rancour.

During the late forties and early fifties, my parents began employing a procession of "displaced people" whom the war had uprooted and set adrift. The Yamazakis came first. They were a Japanese couple, middle-aged with young adult children. They had been forcibly uprooted from their peaceful life in British Columbia and sent to a Canadian internment camp. When they were not allowed to return to the West Coast in spite of peace having been declared, they came to Guelph. One of their daughters was a student nurse at the hospital where Mother and Dad worked as doctors.

All through the war, my brothers and sister and I had not been allowed to speak of "Japs" as the other kids did. We were sternly reminded that we had many Japanese friends and that it was wrong to speak so of a people who were already suffering. Mother and Dad also had friends who had perished in Japanese prisoner of war camps but what they endured was not relayed to us until we were grown. Now we were told firmly not to call people without homes DPs, as most people did, but New Canadians.

After the Yamazakis relocated, we met a Latvian family, a Dutch girl younger than I who had been sent away by her mother during the worst fighting in Holland, and a Russian couple. Inevitably, we also met many of their friends and relations. We heard about loneliness, fear, loss, shattered dreams as we did the dishes together or helped make beds. Although I was a self-absorbed teenager who wanted others to listen to my problems and resented having to share my parents' limited time with suffering humanity, I could not help being apalled and moved sometimes to tears by the pain and terror and loss through which these survivors had lived.

Among the people who came to Canada to wash dishes, scrub floors, cut grass, and shovel snow were lawyers, ministers, teachers, and professors. They had little or nothing left of their vanished lives. Always, wherever they went, the shadow of war followed them, diminishing their dreams, stealing their youth, invalidating their education. It was years before most of them felt they belonged in Canada. Some never did.

Then I was old enough to go away to college. During my second year, I picked up a new book called *The Diary of a Young Girl* by Anne Frank. Unaware of her capture, torture, and death, I read along, aching for her in her imprisonment, yet confidently waiting for the war to end and her freedom to be given back to her. When I turned the last page and found out that she never did escape, that all her worst fears came true in scenes of brutality and terror beyond my imagining, I fell apart and wept for hours. The following day, even though I attended classes and worked on essays again, I went about burdened with a horror I could not shake.

Mother had comforted me as a child by repeating, over and over, "Jean, it's only a story. Everything will be all right in the end."

But what had happened to Anne Frank was not just a story. It was a darkness with no stars. Everything went tragically wrong in the end. And this had been brought about by human beings like me. The Nazis who broke in on her hiding place had begun life as tiny babies, had taken their first steps, had been rocked to sleep like me. What had turned them into monsters who could use people so cruelly? What had twisted their humanity out of shape? Could I ever lose mine?

I did not know. I still do not fully understand. But I do know that the movies and books which finish up with the joyous homecoming of the gallant hero, limping only a little, lie. Real war wounds maim you for life. Fear haunts the dreams of children caught in war even when they become grandparents. Although I lived through the war years cocooned in my cosy Canadian childhood, the life stories told to me by people who had survived World War II, and a book written by a teenager who had not, taught me that war has no happy ending. Although I still live in a cocoon called Canada, I try not to forget.

JEAN LITTLE *completed an Honours degree in English at Victoria College, University of Toronto. She became that rarity, a Canadian children's author who earns a living and supports others by her writing. Jean lives with her sister Pat, her grandniece and nephew, and a bevy of pets. Because of her limited vision, she has had to find specialized ways of writing and editing. She types her work on a computer that can then read it back to her. Jean is a prolific writer, quick to seize on an idea, and disciplined in turning it into a successful manuscript. With twenty-seven books published, she has won many Canadian and international awards; three of her books have been made into films. Jean is a member of the Order of Canada. Adjectives like "ardent" and "passionate" describe her. Her heroes move most readers deeply, and her novels, easy readers, picture books, and two volumes of autobiography are treasured by many readers.*

CHRISTOPHER CHAPMAN

In 1939, thousands of miles from the outbreak of war, the lives and fortunes of many Canadian families changed.

A difficult and rocky road developed for my family, which I became aware of as I grew up during those years.

At the outset of World War II, my twin brother, Francis, and I were twelve, and the last of a family of four boys and two girls. Sisters Philippa and Sally stayed home, sharing with us the changes brought on by the war years. Philippa worked with the Red Cross and Sally nursed. My brothers, Howard, 22, and Bob, 18, went to war in very different and opposite ways.

The elder siblings attended private schools. Francis and I began there, too, but Father's financial situation changed dramatically and Francis and I were split up, much to our horror. I was sent to a vocational school to study art. Academics were very difficult for me, and I felt at the time that I was sent to art school as a simple way out. In my diploma year of 1943 I stood third in a class of four. I have never been quite sure what the grade meant as there was so little to measure it by. In my opinion I was showing no signs of any remarkable achievement in the arts. I began to feel conscious of my family's concern as to where I was headed. However, the financial changes brought on by war may have been a well-disguised blessing to my development as an artist. I was scared at times as to my direction, but grateful for not being harassed or unduly pressured. Direction and development came intuitively. I wish my father had lived to see what eventually evolved for me.

I grew up thinking all families were like ours, living in one house. There were Daddy and Mum, Grandmother Ducky, Aunt Beebo, and Aunt Hay Hay. They had proper names but these were the ones we called them. Most of the nicknames originated from my sister Philippa, called Pippa. She was the eldest of my siblings, followed by Howard, Bob, and Sally called Bee. Francis was never referred to as Frank. I was Kit. My mother said she christened me Christopher in order to call me Kit. It was certainly easier for me to spell as I struggled with words like Christopher. An Ojibway maid and a cook also lived in the house, making up part of the family. Two dogs, a canary, and a cat called Mitya Karamazov, Minnie for short, completed the household.

Top Hat Kit.

When war broke out Francis and I were attending a small private school. One of our teachers was a retired British Colonel, a handsome man who, I decided, was created for or by the "Great War." He was one of those kindly, staunch British Imperialists bred to believe, and who fought to maintain that, "Britain ruled the waves" — up until that time. My first experience of seeing a man cry, let alone a proud soldier, happened when news came that Austria had been invaded and had fallen to Germany prior to the declaration of war in 1939. We could tell he knew what was to follow. The Colonel instilled in me an enormous number of stories and now-forgotten knowledge of the First War. I was left, however, with an atmosphere of what World War I meant to someone who had fought in it.

The Colonel became a close friend to Francis and me. It was hard for us to watch this proud man, who had distinguished himself in "the war to end all wars," disintegrate into misery, forgotten except by a very few. He died poverty stricken in a military hospital. I have a book, a prize signed by the Colonel. It was given at our graduation. There seemed to be endless awards. Every student got one, and the final one was for me. There was a short dreamlike moment when I tried to think of what it was for. It was a consolation prize. At first I wasn't sure what the word meant; nevertheless I "prized" it very much.

My father, Alfred Chapman, was a distinguished Toronto architect. We lived in a fine large home on a ravine at the edge of Rosedale, which was (and still is) a fashionable neighbourhood. He designed three houses there: one for his family, one for his parents, and one to accommodate his expanding family after Francis and I were born. The houses were among the first built on a stretch of gravel road, formerly the city dump. Mum called our house The Dumpling.

Even though architectural assignments supported my father through the prewar depression, a new undertaking became an investment disaster that drastically altered the life he had planned. Rather than see his partners suffer, he put up his own money. In other circumstances, he would have recovered, but the war put a stop to his kind of work. His last major architectural project, the Bank of Montreal in downtown Toronto, was already well under construction in the fall of 1939. I marvelled at the beautifully detailed plaster model that stood about six feet tall. Even the great hall could be seen in detail with its many columns to be in polished black granite. The project was suddenly cancelled for "patriotic" reasons. We could not know it at the time, but, in fact, my father's distinguished career ended with the outbreak of war.

Our lives were changed. I remember the sad day the maid and cook had to be let go. They had become part of our family. From then on Mum took over most of the cooking with the help of Aunt Beebo and Grandmother Ducky. As a child I had little idea of the work required to maintain our house, as well as feed the family, friends, and eventual boarders during the war. Our meals consisted of eight to ten family members plus whatever "Guests." There never seemed any let-up of people. The coming and going of so many led one boarder to comment that a total stranger could walk into our home, take a bath, leave again, and we would just grunt an acknowledgement, thinking the person must be a friend of the family or boarder. Wartime made life so different. There was an openness to everyone and everything, a trust of friendship that, looking back as I grew up, seemed natural and wonderful.

In 1940, when the great fear of German invasion of Britain was at its height, there was much discussion over sending children en mass to Canada and other safe countries. Aunt Hay Hay made arrangements to adopt a War Guest. A frightened four-and-a-half-year-old girl was picked up by Hay Hay from the train to be part of our family until the end of the war. The sad little girl was in such distress that Hay Hay took her directly to the cottage on Lake Simcoe. June spent summers at the lake and winters in the city, staying with us when she was not at boarding school, which was only a few minutes walk from our home.

The cottage was on a lakefront portion of the family farm. The farm was rundown when Daddy and Aunt Hay Hay purchased it, and it was not improved by an alcoholic tenant. This created a challenge for our later tenants and for us twins. During the war the farm became an important part of Francis's and my life. Francis got off school early in the spring and became very involved in farm work at $4.00 a week, with many twelve-hour days. We learned how to run the farm horses and equipment, using "gee" and "haw" with the

(left) Twelve-hour days were not unusual at the farm.
(right) My father, Alfred Chapman, was a distinguished Toronto architect.

working horses and "coboss" to call the cows in for milking. I feel if you coax a cow through friendship, she will let you milk her and make you think it is your technique producing the milk. I remember the warm teats on a cold morning limbering my hands and wonder how the cow felt!

Howard was studying architecture when war broke out. He found himself in a difficult position, as the idea of killing conflicted with his Christian beliefs. He became a conscientious objector. I grew to understand what this meant, but was unaware at the time of its stigma and some of the difficulties both Howard and Daddy faced in accepting this direction. If Howard had stayed in Canada while conscription was in force, he probably would have gone to jail rather than go into military service. He found great support in the stand taken by the Society of Friends with respect to war. After working his way to England, he served with the Quaker Friends Ambulance Unit (FAU) until the end of the war.

Howard left us on February 6, 1942, at first to join the Seamen's Pool in Halifax where he was assigned to a fuelling ship. Next he worked on a tramp steamer in a massive convoy to England. In these convoys all ships had to go at the same rate as the slowest ship, making the Atlantic crossings tedious and dangerous. Convoys reminded me of the sheep on the family farm. Adult sheep instinctively herd the young ones together and surround them to protect the lambs from marauding wolves or coyotes, just like the convoys shepherding supplies, people, and troops against the German U-boats.

Howard chose to work in a humanitarian capacity, but we never quite knew where he was located even though he corresponded faithfully. His pay was $7.50 a month.

During the period when Howard, and later Bob, went away I only understood Howard had gone to war in a different way to Bob, who had joined the RCAF. Howard chose to work in a humanitarian capacity in hospitals and refugee camps, but we never quite knew where he was located even though he corresponded faithfully. His letters came from such places as Gaza, Palestine, the islands of Casos, Carpothos, Cairo, and the Island of Rhodes. His FAU pay was $7.50 a month.

My father had a weakness for beautiful cars, which was inherited by his sons. At the time of the war we had a small practical Studebaker and a secondhand 1934 grey Packard convertible. We called it Grey Owl. Bob, while in the air force, found a 1932 Cadillac roadster, one of those wonderful open cars with no glass windows and a rumble seat that swung out to make it a four-passenger. There was a small door on the side just for golf clubs! Gas rationing forced the Packard into storage, and when Bob went to war, his car, named Galloping Gus Guzzling Gas, was also put into storage.

(above) "Grey Owl" — twins and Sally on the back.

(below) Bob's "Gus."

During Bob's embarkation leave we went to see the George Formby film *It's in the Air*. Formby was an English North Country banjo-playing comedian turning out large numbers of slapstick comedy films. They took Britain by storm and helped take their audience's minds off the Blitz and the threat of German invasion. His giddy films were a great success in Canada as well. Bob and I roared our way through *It's in the Air*. I was fifteen years old. I will never forget Bob's wild enjoyment, and my own.

Not long after that happy evening we all went down to Union Station, an imposing edifice of stone and space, to see Bob off to war. I recall the impression of thousands of men and women pouring through that huge cave of a building, shuffling and running feet, weeping goodbyes, and the jumble of words crackling and echoing over the PA system with information I could hardly decipher. I remember sombre colours of fat dunnage bags, blue-grey and khaki, the smell of service uniforms, tobacco smoke, and whiffs of perfume along with steam trains waiting and hissing. This mixture of sounds and smells left an indelible memory. Then, the final river of brown and blue disappearing into the tunnels of the station.

Bob was on his way to what? For a moment I choked. Suddenly a distant face in that grey mass turned and smiled. He could not wave being laden down with baggage, but there he was and we were waving like mad. Bob gave us confidence he knew what he was doing. He was part of the patriotic hype of soldier, sailor, airman going off to battle. I don't think I really grasped it all or what the country seemed to be doing or supporting. The contrast between Bob's departure and Howard's was significant. Howard had slipped away to find his own part in the war.

Eric Aldwinckle was a close friend of the family. An artist of many talents, he distinguished himself as an RCAF war artist, adding to the remarkable and moving collection of individual painters' impressions of war, now stored in the bowels of Ottawa. Before going overseas, Eric took Francis and me on our first canoe trip into Georgian Bay. Two fourteen-year-olds and Eric, with all their goods and chattels, canoed and camped through the islands out from Little Current. It was 1941, and as we drove towards White Fish Falls we were stopped by a parade of escorted German prisoners of war, out for a march from their nearby camp. The officers were in uniform. The men were marching with precision and singing heartily. It was a bizarre experience, like a scene from a film. We were told that a two-hundred-foot tunnel they had been digging for escape had recently been discovered. Escape to where? There was a sense of victory in the gusto with which they were singing. It was strangely impressive. At that early time of the war they must have felt it was theirs to win.

On a cold January night in 1943, the family had just returned from seeing the movie *The Goose Steps In.* Aunt Hay Hay was preparing cocoa and we were all gathered in the kitchen discussing the film, the memory of which has left me. The doorbell rang. It was eleven o'clock. We fell silent as my father went to the door, followed by Mum. In the silence we heard the door close and a moment later we heard Daddy say in a low tone, "This is it." These words, their meaning slowly realized, have stayed with me for a lifetime. "Regret to inform you advice has been received from the Royal Canadian Air Force Casualties Office overseas that . . ."

Bob had been killed. There was a numbing emptiness, then hugs and tears, but tears suppressed by the adults. I do not remember Daddy coming to us. A man did not show his tears: it was a sign of weakness and fathers don't cry, or so we were told. Looking back, I hope he allowed himself to cry.

The large house was strangely empty as if Bob had just left, instead of nine months earlier. Withdrawing from the quiet devastation downstairs, Francis and I climbed to the attic and our beds. I paused along the way to say goodnight to June, and stayed with her for a few moments. June asked me, "Why couldn't Bob just jump out of the plane before it hit the ground?"

Mum came up to the attic and cried with us. We thought of Howard who was somewhere in England unaware. Mum left and we stared at the dark ceiling and the play of car lights going by. I thought of the monumental letter I had written to Bob, which he never received. At sixteen it was hard for me to realize how important letters were to those away at war. Instead of writing shorter letters and more of them, I had written eleven pages that were lost en route to England. It saddened me and I've lived with that regret for a lifetime. The real horror of war was a long way off, but a very personal part had stabbed us deeply. The next morning Father went to the office and Mum went to Woman's College Hospital to tell Sally, who was in training as a nurse. The shock to her was overwhelming.

As I lay in bed that night the distant image of Bob smiling before he disappeared into Union Station became vivid and it has never left my memory. Maybe if Bob had returned to us after the war that memory would no longer be so necessary. But it was my last image of him. For a while after Bob's death I kept his picture in my locker at school. Gradually as Francis and I grew older, we passed the age of Bob's at twenty-one. Now we are in our seventies and he is still twenty-one.

Following Bob's death, Mum (who had written plays for all her young children to perform) wrote a short story about an air man and I designed a cover for the little book. There is no reference to Bob's name but those who know feel he is there. The story is like a dream, and in it is a brief conversation with a young air man and his mother:

"You don't mind, do you?" he asked, "that I am glad to go?"

She replied, "I am glad for you if you are glad."

Bob was a romantic and he made his choice. Mother and Father along with others in the family had the love and courage to support it. I am sure the quote mentioned in Mum's story applied to Howard's decision as well as Bob's. I wished it might have been the same for Daddy.

Following the devastating news, sketchy information filtered in to our family about what had happened. Bob was a navigator assigned to a Royal Air Force Lancaster bomber squadron on North Atlantic air service. The aircraft named *V for Victory* with a crew of seven ran into difficulty after the pilot radioed a request to land at a nearby airstrip. "Something" went wrong. The rear gunner Norman was able to bail out and to his horror watched the aircraft go down, taking his chums to their death.

The crew members were extremely close. All but Bob were from England. Their squadron leader wrote my father about Bob's funeral. He was buried at the village of Brigg in Lincolnshire, not far from where they crashed. Bob was given full honours. Members of the RAF carried the casket draped with the Union Jack and provided the firing party. The Last Post was sounded. There was something consoling about this ceremony, one amid thousands going on during war. Bob and his crew joined the 21,000 young men of the Royal Air Force Bomber Command who lost their lives.

The one surviving member of the crew could not write to us in detail at the time because of wartime censorship. Norman, age nineteen, was listed as missing three months later. Five months after that his personal belongings were returned to his mother. Such a terrible, final gesture after the agony of waiting.

My family received this poem:

"In affectionate remembrance of — Bill,
Bob, Ron, Eric, Tony and Brad from their
Rear Air Gunner Norman"

Eastward they climb — black shapes
against the grey of falling dusk,
Gone with the nodding day
from the English field.

Bob in London.

Not theirs the sudden glow of triumph
that their fighter brothers know:
Only to fly through cloud, through storm,
through night, unerring, and to keep
their purpose bright.

Nor turn until, their dreadful duty done,
Westward they climb to race the awakened sun.

The following are excerpts from Bob's last letter, which arrived a couple of days after the news of his death:

January 15 & 20, 1943

Dear Mum and Daddy:

. . . Can you stand some plain facts for a minute. Please don't

forget that if anything happens to me — no matter what, I shall always be with you. That life which we have all enjoyed so much is certainly worth doing anything for . . . I have wanted to speak freely for some time and never did.

Should anything happen — I am perfectly confident it won't — please don't grieve. It could be no other way. By the way I don't hate the prospect of being a prisoner of war to any great extent . . . cheer up, I hope I shouldn't be sorry for letting you know this.

The letter continues:

How cheering the news is, Rommel is on the run again . . . I sometimes wonder if some miraculous thing isn't going to happen to finish this war very suddenly . . . Last night Bill and Eric and I went into [censored] and saw Walt Disney's Bambi. *What a beautiful piece of work. Everyone should see it. It absolutely held me spellbound in spots. The music is grand too.*

Please ask the twins to write — I get such a kick out of their letters . . . Hope they had a nice birthday.

All my Love to you both, Bob

Not long after the incident, our war artist friend, Eric, went to Bob's gravesite and painted a beautiful watercolour, which he sent to my parents.

As I grew older and the bombing raids on Germany increased to incredible numbers, I wondered how bomber crews could steel themselves against the horror they had to inflict in so many cases on civilians: a terrifying fact of war. One of the songs we used to sing with great gusto at campfires and corn roasts was, "Praise the Lord and pass the ammunition, and we'll all be free." I grew to hate it.

One day a young man came to our door. He had a flat tire and no tools or spare. We had tools so I was able to help remove the wheel, take the tire off the rim, and patch the inner tube. The man was on leave from the air force. He was a bomber pilot and had survived many missions on RCAF Lancasters, which was a feat in itself. As he talked to me about "Lanks" and his part in the war, he helped me connect to Bob. Twice we repaired the flat and twice it did not hold air. Finally he was on his way — for how long on those tires I wondered, as he disappeared out of sight. Tubes and tires were difficult to get in wartime. As he left, he said he would bring me a model of the "Lank" he had made. I never saw him again, but that meeting and conversation were special in my memory.

As the devastating cloud over Bob's death lifted a little, my father was motivated to help make the farm really work. He drew up plans to renovate the large barn from a quagmire of rot to an efficient structure. It all looked positive and exciting. Within a few days of finishing his plans, he suffered a paralytic stroke, and, despite our best efforts, the dream sputtered out. We had good farm tenants, but Francis and I were only there to help in the summer. The farm produced its share of goods: chickens, eggs, some beef, sheep, lambs, hay, potatoes, some milk, ducks, turkeys, and Hay Hay's honey. Francis raised mushrooms and had a special interest in the goats. It all sounds a bit grand but it was done under much difficulty for the farmer and his wife. There was no electricity for the farm until after the war.

Daddy's stroke was devastating for all of us. He was a quiet, gentle man, who struggled to be independent of his affliction. Unable to speak and half paralyzed, he was eventually able to take shuffling walks, but never recovered enough to put sentences together — he could not even read. When he had something on his mind, we would gather around and enact a game like charades. We created images or drawings that would lead to his nodding approval. It was always something of importance and well thought out. Jigsaw puzzles and picture books were his pastime. He could beat us all at Chinese Checkers. I have always felt his stroke was caused in part by the serious financial worries we knew little about at the time, and by his inability to let go and express his real loss with Bob's death.

Mum knew nothing about how to handle Father's affairs. At first, she was sure we were now destitute. To make things worse, the doctor would not sign the insurance papers for compensation as my father had the use of "at least" one arm and one leg. The fact that he could not read, write, or talk was not considered. It meant no insurance claim could be made even though Father was shrouded in a world he was unable to express. It was this way for over six years. His funeral in 1949 was enormous, a recognition of him and his remarkable architectural legacy.

I have always regretted not knowing my father more intimately. In those days I guess our relationship was not unusual. Fathers were those who went to work, looked after finances, and saw everything necessary for the family was done. At least this is how I grew up. His stroke came at a critical time. Francis and I were sixteen and just becoming aware of the enormous load on Mother. One beautiful gesture after Father's stroke was the arrival of flowers from Holy Blossom Temple, one of his last buildings. They came every year until his death.

Mum had been a concert pianist. Her playing meant so much to all of us, but it too, suffered in the new life before her. Aunt Beebo taught violin to students in our home and at schools. (She also tutored me with my general school work.) The Bechstein concert grand piano, given as a wedding present by my father, was a symbol in our lives of the music that came forth through my mother, Pippa, and, to a lesser degree, Sally. Howard played the cello and Francis played the violin. I was the only one of the children who did not continue with music education. Sometimes I wonder why, since I am devoted to the classics and loved the house filled with music by family, friends, and visitors. One hundred people once gathered for a concert in our music room.

Before Howard went overseas he selected a wartime car for the family, a 1941 two-door Hudson sedan. It served us well. The last year cars were made in North America until the end of the war was 1942. As the war continued, all kinds of older cars were put back into service, but parts were difficult to get. We were allowed to buy additional gas because of the farm. Without this extra ration I figured we could only travel up to six miles a day.

After some searching, Francis and I found a "tractor" for the farm consisting of a Model A Ford front end attached to a truck rear end. Francis named it the Cadillactor. The machine was a very moody half or triple breed, but when the farm horse Old Tom was struck by lightning it filled in for his loss. We searched for a farm truck, again a difficult thing to find in wartime, particularly for the inexperienced. To fill the gap, Bob's Galloping Gus was taken out of storage, becoming a temporary and most impractical farm vehicle. The only thing going for it was four working wheels. Carrying the things a farm vehicle is asked to carry was awkward, to say the least, for a roadster with no windows, especially for the tenants in winter.

We eventually found a truck, though it, too, gave us problems. There was now no reason to keep Bob's car and Mother sold it. The idea of putting Gus away somewhere for the duration was not considered. The sale was a great disappointment, but I had to believe it was necessary. I felt for Mum; it must have been difficult for her to part with Bob's Galloping Gus. The Packard was also sold. Mother could not get much for it because of gas rationing, although it was a classy automobile. This was another sad parting. My film projector and Francis's microscope were sold as well.

The twins — Christopher (me, alias Kit) and Francis.

By this time Francis and I had our driving licences. The Hudson became a great hauler for the farm after I found I could remove the back seat. One of my notes from 1944 reads: "Trip to city in Hudson — 5 sacks of apples, 1 sack of duck feathers, 1 sack of potatoes, 2 garbage cans of manure and a 15 gallon barrel of cider. Plus two passengers and driver." The Hudson was also used to transport a billy goat to Toronto for delivery to a customer, but the customer was not around and so the goat stayed with us in the city.

Billy disappeared, causing great pandemonium.

Anyone who knows billy goats understands one needs a great deal of fresh air when travelling with them and, for that matter, for weeks afterwards. Billy disappeared, causing great pandemonium. We all went out to search for him. One gentleman waiting for the bus was approached by my mother. Asked if he had seen a goat, he was quite taken aback since he lived in a very "respectable part of town." He made it clear there could be no goats in Rosedale, even during wartime. Eventually we found Billy enjoying someone's garden.

The Royal Family became an important symbol during the war. They meant much to our family. I will never forget King George's halting speeches with long pauses between words as he struggled with a crippling stutter. He wound his way into our hearts giving courage to his people with love and dignity, just as Churchill did with power and eloquence. The Queen would occasionally speak and in 1940 Princess Elizabeth, then fourteen, made her first broadcast. (She is one year older than I am.) Even the awful static on these important overseas broadcasts added to their drama. The CBC came into its own during that period and through it the BBC also entered our homes.

Grandmother Ducky, with failing eyesight, depended on the CBC for Anglican Church broadcasts and news so painful about her beloved England. Her letters to England were difficult but she always struggled to keep her contacts there.

In January 1945 Francis and I turned eighteen, the age to join up. The war had gone on for almost six years. It seemed impossible for Germany to survive the mass destruction by land and air much longer. Francis and I had been considering what we should do. During the war years we attended some Quaker meetings and our direction lent towards following Howard. Perhaps we, too, could help people suffering from the war.

Howard's decision seemed very definite and clear-cut. I will always admire him for it, but I have to admit my mind was not that clear. Killing was on a scale never before imagined. Howard's path was an alternative. I still had little idea of the stigma attached to pacifism and was unaware that my move in this direction might hurt my father. He had been upset by Howard's choice but perhaps the long-drawn-out war softened his feelings towards pacifism. How I wished I could have discussed it with him.

My decision never had to be made, however, since conscription was cancelled. The war was coming to an end. The romance of going to war that had captured Bob and so many others was leaching away. Duty to one's country and freedom were the driving forces. I believe duty applies to humanitarian services as well as to fighting.

There was an explosion of rejoicing on May 7 when Germany surrendered. For a moment I felt I had just walked out of a black-and-white film and colour was returning to the world, but then the full impact of suffering and devastation dawned on me. The colours paled.

Two days after the war ended in Europe a telegram from June's parents arrived: "Want June back to peaceful England." And so after five years June returned home with a general proficiency prize from school. She was nine and a half. We thought it would be wonderful for her to go back home and did not realize the extent to which our home and family had become hers, more than her own in England and the baby brother she had never seen. As time went on, we learned how difficult it was for her to adjust.

The mist that had shrouded us for six years was beginning to lift. Lights once dimmed or turned off came on, speed limits rose. Rationing eased for both gas and food, except for essentials like meat, which was in short supply because so much was sent overseas.

A week before Germany surrendered, Mum cabled one hundred dollars to Howard for his return passage. Because Howard was a civilian he was unable to book space until almost a year later. Even then he needed the help of the Canadian High Commissioner in London, Vincent Massey. It was a long wait but on hearing Howard had landed in New York and would be home in literally hours I wrote, "It's still too wonderful to believe." He arrived home on February 22, 1946, six months after Japan surrendered.

Like so many who were away during the war years, Howard did not find it easy to re-enter the life he had left behind. Everything had changed in so many ways. Even though Father was unable to speak, Howard's return must have been a very great joy and pride in his life. Howard had done what he believed in and not taken up arms against anyone. That's the way I felt.

The Lancaster bomber mounted near the CNE is a reminder of Bob — and the thousands of other young airmen who lost their lives.

On Toronto's waterfront beside the Canadian National Exhibition is a Lancaster bomber mounted on a concrete pedestal. To a boy this plane was exciting to see but later I would shudder, for it symbolized a mixture of technical achievement, courage, and the horror of war. Now the CNE Lancaster is slowly disintegrating and where it once looked huge (and was for its day) it now looks small and vulnerable. On one side and overlooking this wartime symbol stand the towering Princes' Gates designed by my father in a competition in 1927, the year I was born.

Designed by Dad, the towering Princes' Gates stand close enough to watch over "Bob's" disintegrating Lancaster.

CHRISTOPHER CHAPMAN *became an artist in film, honoured in Canada and internationally for his ground-breaking work. His first film,* The Seasons, *won the 1954 Canadian Film of the Year, as well as several international awards. Since then, this self-taught filmmaker has created major works for expositions, production companies, corporations, and governments, winning an Oscar for* A Place to Stand *(Expo '67). Christopher's many awards include the first Ontario Film Institute award, for his "distinguished achievements and significant contribution to the development of the Canadian film." He is a member of the Order of Canada. More recently, Christopher has turned his innovative eye towards the Reflected Image, using his still camera to produce mural size photographic images, which have been exhibited in Canada and Europe. Writing this chapter has stimulated Christopher to work on his autobiography, recording in words some of his adventures in filmmaking. "My experiences," he states, "have been rich, frustrating, exciting, fulfilling, and sometimes terrifying."*

Monica Hughes

I sometimes wonder: What if the war had never happened?

September 1939 changed my life in more ways than I could have imagined at the time. I was thirteen years old that summer before the war, and my sister, Liz, was twelve. We were living in Edinburgh, Scotland, and Dad had decided that we would have our first family holiday abroad, in Switzerland — that we were old enough to appreciate it and not be a nuisance. In honour of the occasion, Mum bought me a long dress to wear for dinner at the hotel and for our evening walks along the promenade beside Lake Lucerne. It was of pale yellow taffeta with a net overskirt and a frill around the bottom, and I felt incredibly sophisticated and grown-up. It was the first — and the last — pretty dress I was to own in seven years.

We children didn't read the paper or listen to the radio; we were "protected" from what was going on in the world outside the immediate circle of home and school, so we were really unaware of the political situation in Europe. On our holiday, though, we saw soldiers drilling in the streets — "not to fight," we were told, "but to protect Switzerland in case of war."

War! The word sparked our imaginations. My sister and I talked secretly about how exciting it would be if this "war" should happen while we

Our first family holiday abroad, in Lucerne, Switzerland, turned out to be our last.

were on holiday. Suppose we were trapped in this beautiful country of mountains, lakes, and delicious food for the duration? What a prospect! Especially the food.

Every day we had elegant pastries, ice creams, and water ices in flavours we had never encountered before, meats and fish in wonderful sauces, strange and delicious little munchies that were called "hors d'oeuvres." I was a skinny child and had always been a picky eater, but the wonderful and varied dishes we ate in Switzerland stimulated my tastebuds in ways that the rice puddings and bread-and-milk suppers of home never had. I was also in a growth spurt, growing taller by the moment, and it was ironic that my new teenage appetite would soon have so little to satisfy it.

To the disappointment of Liz and me, and the relief of our parents, we arrived home safely in Edinburgh, early in August, at the end of our Swiss tour. While we'd been away things had changed. Our local park had been carved into trenches for anti-aircraft guns. Everyone was being fitted with gas masks, ugly black things with snouts that made us look like fierce pigs and smelt horribly of rubber. When mine was fastened tightly over my head, I could hear my breath roaring in my ears. It was a scary feeling, and I wondered: *Will I ever have to use this?* The masks came in cardboard boxes that were supposed to be slung over our shoulders and carried everywhere "in the event of war."

Churchman's Cigarettes printed this card showing civilians the proper way to wear their gas masks.

The idea of "war" still didn't seem real. There was a lot of talk among the grown-ups about Danzig and the "Polish corridor," which the Nazis were threatening; but the immediacy of danger made little impression on my sister and me. Until that fatal Sunday, September 3.

We went to church as usual and came home to our regular Sunday breakfast of grilled sausages. These were the Sunday treat, after six days of porridge, and they were expertly grilled by my father (his one and only cooking feat). The radio was on — very unusual, as Dad would not tolerate any "noise." It was then that we heard the news that, since Germany had invaded Poland two days earlier and had not responded to warnings from Great Britain and France, we were officially at war.

It seemed only moments later that the air raid sirens began to wail, an alien warbling that gave me shivers down my spine and butterflies in my stomach. We all ran upstairs to the drawing room, where the large bay windows gave us a clear view to the south and east, and we stared out. Would we see hundreds of Nazi planes darkening the sky, coming to invade us from across the North Sea?

It was a glorious autumn day, and there was nothing to see but a clear blue sky. Dad suddenly realized the danger of all that glass, should planes appear and bombs begin to fall, and he tried to close the inside shutters. These shutters had fascinated Liz and me when we first moved into the big old granite house four years earlier. They were stored in panels on either side of the windows; when the panels were opened they could be unfolded right across the glass and secured with iron bars.

Mum had had heavy velvet curtains installed and the shutters had never been used, much to our disappointment. Closing shutters and fastening iron bars would have been like living in a castle under siege, I had thought, much more exciting than just drawing curtains at night.

Now, as Dad unfolded the big panels, I felt as if we *were* under siege. To his frustration he couldn't get them to close properly. Liz and I watched. The idea of us barricading ourselves into our own house was both exciting and very scary. We looked at each other in silent anticipation. So this was war! Whatever was going to happen next?

Then the "all-clear" sounded, a high note that for years was to be associated with the reprieve from danger — until the next time. The sun went on shining in the empty blue sky. It had been a false alarm. The shutters were folded away and, indeed, they were never used, as Mum's heavy velvet curtains made a most adequate "blackout."

It was then that Mum and Dad told us what had only been a rumour among our friends. Plans had already been made for our small convent school to be evacuated "in the event of war." We were to leave on Monday: the next day! Our clothes were hastily packed and all was ready.

"Don't make us go," we begged. "We won't be any trouble, honestly." But Mum told us that Edinburgh was considered an "invasion port" which the German fleet, steaming across the North Sea, might attack. This was terrible. What if we left home and never saw our parents again? Suppose there *was* an invasion; suppose they were killed? "Not everyone is going," we pleaded. "Maureen's staying." But our pleadings were in vain. Mum and Dad were kind but firm, and their faces gave us no indication of what they must have been feeling — that they might miss us every bit as much as we would miss them.

Next morning we walked down the street to the school, our gas masks over our shoulders, with hardly time to realize what was going to happen. Our friends were standing there with their parents; the small ones in the lower school were to leave later. We looked at each other without a word. I think all of us were afraid of bursting into tears. I know my stomach was full of butterflies, a strange mixture of fear and anticipation.

Dad taught a morning class at the university, so we hugged Mum and kissed her goodbye. Then, reluctantly, we climbed aboard the coach and watched as it pulled away from the familiar school and headed west into the unknown. *When would we be back?* I wondered.

We stopped for a sandwich lunch somewhere in the middle of Scotland, and then headed westward towards the fishing port of Oban. The sun sparkled on the blue water, and the fishing boats out in the bay bobbed at their moorings, as if this were an ordinary holiday outing. But there was something unreal about this postcard beauty; this was no holiday. We were running away. Escaping from unknown danger.

The coach headed south along a winding road, with glimpses on our right of a wild rocky shoreline and the ocean beyond. In the middle of nowhere the coach suddenly stopped and we all got off. From here we were to walk through the grounds of the estate where we would be living, while the coach took the long steep way round with all our luggage aboard.

We trudged past rocks covered with black seaweed on our right and meadows of rough grass on our left, where fierce-looking Highland cattle, with shaggy coats and huge horns like bicycle handles, glared at us as if we were unwelcome intruders.

At last the road left the shore and led us uphill through a gloomy thicket of rhododendron, spooky and unfriendly. *Maybe it would be brighter in the spring when the bushes were in flower*, I thought. Then I thought: *Spring? Surely the war will be over by spring and we'll be safely home. By Christmas, some people had said.*

We came out of the shadowy plantation of rhododendrons into sunshine again, onto a small plateau on which was perched the most romantic house I had ever seen. *Not like a school. More like a castle*, I marvelled, *with its stone turrets and stepped gables.* We were told that it was a hunting lodge, called Lunga House, lent to the school by Lord Lindsay, the head of the clan MacDougall.

A door as big as the entrance to a cathedral fronted the building, and above it was a crest carved in stone, with the clan motto in Gaelic. Inside was a huge hall, a ballroom with a dais for the band, and a wide wooden staircase winding up past stag heads and banners into the shadows above.

The organization by nuns and parents must have been immense, but we kids took it for granted. As if by magic, there were our very own beds lined up in rows in the ballroom and in some of the bedrooms upstairs, while other bedrooms were assigned to the different classes. Over the next few days they would be filled with the familiar desks and textbooks. There were even blackboards.

The new arrivals at Lunga House. I am sitting in the second row, just to the right of the priest.

Since there was no electricity, light was supplied by kerosene lamps. As September turned into October and the evenings grew darker, we had to do our homework by lamplight. The "blackout" was a constant preoccupation. Not a single ray of light must ever shine out of the windows of Lunga House, for there might be Nazi submarines lurking in the waters offshore, and a careless light would "aid and abet" the enemy.

In dry spells the water supply was chancy, depending on rainwater collected in the bog at the hilltop behind the school. I had always loved soaking in a boiling hot bath with a book to read and no interruptions. Now baths were strictly limited, with no more than three inches of water, marked at the tap end with a painted line.

As the days went by we began to be less homesick. The ordinary rhythm of classes, homework, field hockey, and tennis, as well as occasional hikes through the countryside to look at some prehistoric site, filled the time. There was a piano in the old ballroom and we sometimes had singsongs in the evenings.

There were also useful war-effort outings: gathering sphagnum moss from the edges of the bog, to be used as an antiseptic dressing for wounded soldiers (there were no antibiotics in those days), and picking rosehips for rosehip and carrot jam to replace the vitamins we would be short of, now that merchant ships could no longer bring tropical crops such as oranges and bananas from around the world. We never saw another banana until the war was over, and oranges were like gold.

By Christmastime the war was *not* over. The battleship *Royal Oak* had been sunk by a U-boat right inside the harbour of Scapa Flow, in the Orkneys; and Nazi battleships and U-boats lurked in the grey waters of the Atlantic, preying on the merchant ships bringing essential supplies to the British Isles. It seemed that the waters washing the shore near the school were more dangerous than anything that might be happening in Edinburgh.

"Please let us come home," we pleaded in our letters to Mum and Dad. Christmas had always been a very special event in our family, starting with church in the morning, followed by a turkey dinner, a plum pudding, and exotic delicacies such as Carlsbad plums, stem ginger in syrup, dried muscatel raisins, sugared almonds, and real Turkish delight. Since, for the rest of the year, our diet was exceedingly boring, with few if any treats, this had always been a season to remember.

On Christmas afternoon, stuffed with good food, we would sit around the drawing room fire, while Mum and Dad handed out parcels from all the great-aunts and uncles. The white candles on the Christmas tree would be lit, and we would sit in the darkening room watching their magic flickering. Then we would have tea, with Christmas cake and Scottish shortbread, and Dad would read aloud to us from his favourite books.

"Please let us come home!" we begged. But the answer was, "No, it's still not safe," and we had to spend Christmas at school. The nuns did their best to entertain us. We had a costume party, and we all dressed up in whatever we could lay our hands on. I wore a smart pair of slacks belonging to my best friend, while she draped a flowered quilt around her like a crinoline and we went as Queen Victoria and Prince Albert.

After Christmas ordinary life resumed. As food shortages grew more intense, we grew hungrier. I expect the nuns did their best, but the food was often awful — burned, lumpy porridge for breakfast, and vegetables that hadn't been properly cleaned. "Just a little extra protein!" we were told gaily if we made a fuss about the slugs nestled in the kale. Dessert was often stewed plums or rhubarb, puckering our mouths, since there wasn't sufficient sugar to make them palatable.

I was always hungry. I had been placed at the very bottom of the long table that filled the dining room, supposedly to keep order among the small ones. By the time the plates of food reached the bottom of the table, the nun in charge was offering "seconds" to her cronies at the top. But second helpings never reached my end. I used to dream of food, dreams in which I would sit down at a table laden with good things; then, just as I was reaching out for a mouthful, I would wake up. Was I remembering that wonderful month in Switzerland?

Luckily for my sister and me, though I didn't feel lucky at the time, I had injured my knee in the first weeks at Lunga. It was painful and swelled up dramatically, and I couldn't play sports or walk far. The old-fashioned country doctor had no suggestions, and the nuns tried several homemade treatments, like iodine, which burned my skin.

Finally a young doctor, standing in as a locum for the old man, visited the school, took one look at my grapefruit-sized knee, and said it should be X-rayed and treated properly. So, joy of joys, Liz and I had to go home for Easter. Even though I spent part of the holiday in hospital, having my knee operated on, it was worth it to be *home*, to know that Mum and Dad were all right, and that nothing dreadful had happened to them while we were away.

Our parents were more than dismayed when they saw us. Not only had my knee been mistreated, but poor Liz was infested with head lice. The previous term a few very young village children had appeared in the school, bringing with them these unwelcome guests. The epidemic had cleared up, except for Liz, whose beautiful wavy hair grew to her waist. Mum had to cut it all off. It was then, I guess, that Mum and Dad began thinking of a new school for us in the fall.

Back at Lunga House for the spring term of 1940, we rejoiced in the wonderful hot weather. It was warm enough to bathe in the sea on May 5, the "feast-day" of the principal, and we all got sunburnt. We played only in the shallows, because the ocean tides could be dangerous, and, between the islands of Scarba and Jura, we could see the line that marked the notorious *Corrievreken*, a huge whirlpool that formed at the turning of the tides, powerful enough — we were told — to suck boats down into its depths, an awesome thought!

The whirlpool was not the only awesome place. On the shore, not far from the lodge, was a standing stone. Like the great circle at Stonehenge and similar stones scattered around England and Scotland, it had been placed there thousands of years earlier, in stone-age times.

Standing all alone near the shore, ancient and mysterious, it gave me the shivers. I cannot explain why I found it so scary. It was not just its age. I had seen many ancient places, but none affected me as did the standing stone at Lunga.

(Long after my schooldays, the memory of that mysterious stone still haunted me. Years later, when I began writing for young people, the standing stone was in my mind, like a dream that wouldn't go away. Finally, in 1995, I was able to write it out, in a story called *The Seven Magpies*, about an imaginary girl evacuated to a strange school in the western Highlands in 1939 . . .)

For my class, the school year of 1940 finished with the Oxford Junior Certificate exam, the first of the hurdles we had to jump on the way to completing our education. And then we went home to Edinburgh, now considered as safe as anywhere could be in wartime. It was evident that Germany was not going to invade Britain by sea; the whole enemy thrust was in the aerial bombing of the south of England and attempts to destroy the merchant ships that were bringing essential foodstuffs and war materials across the Atlantic from Canada and the United States.

There were more shortages, more food rationing, and even clothes rationing. We needed coupons for almost everything, and there were long lines outside the grocery store, the baker, the butcher, because food was not always available, even when you had the coupons for it.

The ration book was even more essential than the gas mask. Every month we were told what our different coupons entitled us to: a tiny piece of meat for a family of four, perhaps an egg or two a week — later, I remember, we were reduced to an egg per person every month. Sugar, butter, and margarine were rationed. Milk was kept for children and expectant mothers. Canned goods were on "points" and very difficult to get. Those people with friends and relatives in North America might get food parcels, but we were not among the lucky ones.

It was when we left Lunga for the summer holidays that Mum and Dad told us that we were going to another school. Young people today would be bewildered by the fact that "back then" children were not involved in any discussions or decision-making. Just as we had not known till the last minute that we were being sent to the west of Scotland, so now we didn't know till just before we went home that we were to be sent to a boarding school in Harrogate, Yorkshire.

Mum had received from the school an enormous list of essential clothing, and she spent every spare moment making our dresses. Light blue for everyday wear in summer, with white on Sundays. Navy skirts and blouses in winter, with mid-blue wool dresses trimmed with maroon for Sundays. Gym tunics and new underwear to be bought. I don't know how she managed it all.

Finally, in September 1940, we caught the train from Edinburgh to York and waited for a local train to nearby Harrogate, a journey of about five hours altogether, though this was to vary, we found. When the bombing in the south of England was severe, trains were often delayed.

The convent was a beautiful building on the outskirts of the old city. It was scary facing a new school and strangers, but I felt better when one of the nuns waiting to welcome us gave me a big hug. "So you're the young lady who got distinction in maths!"

The warmth of our welcome, the beauty of the chapel and the great main staircase, the smell of freshly waxed floors, the orderliness of the life, and the quality of the teaching were all balm to my soul. For a while my sister and I slept in the dormitories, each bed curtained in white for privacy; but before long we were assigned a private room together, which was wonderful.

The food was well cooked, and, in spite of rationing, there was always enough to eat. The midmorning snack was bread and "dripping," the fat saved from cooking bacon or beef. It tasted wonderful and was very filling, and back then cholesterol had not been labelled as bad. There was no butter to spare for snacks, so dripping was a great substitute, and bread had not yet been rationed, though later all baked goods were on points.

Did we think about the war? It was always there in the background — *The Times* was on the table in the library, and we were brought up to date on important events — but, in fact, the schoolwork, games, and the occasional breaks to visit historical sites in the neighbourhood, with picnics including the best dark treacly gingerbread I have ever tasted, all these seemed much more important in our daily lives.

Then the air raids began. Historic Harrogate was never a target, but squadrons of Luftwaffe planes droned overhead on their way to bomb Leeds, which was an important manufacturing city. At the warbling sound of the sirens we would traipse downstairs from our warm beds to the safety of the cellar. This was no comfortable modern basement, but only a wide passage that contained the heating system and gave access to the water and drainage pipes, which were right above us. I used to wonder what would happen if a stray bomb *did* hit the school: would all the pipes break and shower water and waste down on our heads?

Sometimes the alerts were of short duration, but at other times they would drag on through the night, while we sat huddled in dressing gowns and blankets, trying to sleep sitting upright on the long benches that lined the walls. After those nights we were allowed to sleep in an extra hour, instead of getting up for early Mass in the convent chapel; the unexpected change to our timetable made these occasions interesting.

Outfitting us for the new school, just at the time when clothes rationing had come into effect, had used up all the family clothes coupons. In my second year at Harrogate, my navy skirt wore out and became indecently thin across the seat. Mum couldn't get me a new one, and for the rest of that winter I had to wear my gym tunic instead of the proper uniform. It was deeply embarrassing for a self-conscious sixteen-year-old, but I never let on I cared. There were other things to worry about.

When we went home for the Christmas holidays in 1941, Dad was ill. He took all sorts of strange-looking medicines and spent much of his time sitting by the gas fire in his study. When Mum met us up at the train station she warned us, "Your father's lost a lot of his hair. Don't talk about it. It'll only upset him."

It snowed that Christmas, which was unusual, and I wanted to clear off the front walk, but Dad chose to do it himself. I began to sulk, but Mum took me aside and gently said, "It'll make him feel better to be doing something. Let him."

I stopped my sulk, but I had an upset, butterflies-in-the-stomach feeling. Something was different and I didn't know what. Dad had always been a very stern and private person; Liz and I were both afraid of him. He was a very clever mathematician, who'd published books and won gold medals for his work. He didn't understand children, and he hated noise of any kind, especially when he was working in his study. I don't remember ever *starting* a conversation with him. He would ask me about school work and sometimes talk to me about the stars — astronomy was one of his passions. So were books, and the upside of this unapproachable man was that he shared this love with us, reading aloud every Sunday afternoon throughout our childhood.

He came back, exhausted but more cheerful from clearing the snow off the sidewalks, to have afternoon tea by the fire. I happened to be standing behind him, looking down on his head, once covered with thick black hair. Impulsively I bent down and kissed his bald head. I was surprised at my temerity. And I suppose he was surprised, too, for he said, "So you do love your old dad, do you?"

The Christmas holidays over, we went back to school. In March 1942, Mum sent Liz and me a letter, telling us that Dad was very ill and in hospital, and that we should pray for him. We clung to each other and longed to be at home, not hundreds of miles away.

A week later, on March 16, the day before St. Patrick's, the principal, Mother Denis, called me out of class. *What was wrong?* My heart thumped as I ran downstairs after her. Liz was waiting on the floor below. Once we were together Mother Denis told us that our father was dead. She then suggested that we spend the rest of the day in our bedroom instead of back in class.

Alone, we stared bleakly at each other and out of the window, where the Yorkshire landscape was wintry, muddy, and grey. *Our father dead? What was going to happen?* Later that day Mum phoned the principal, who told us that Mum didn't want us to go home for the funeral, but that she would come and stay at the convent for a few days afterwards.

"Why can't we go home?" we begged, but Mother Denis's face was stern. "It's what your mother wants. And you must be brave girls." So, of course, we were. We survived the jollity and the games of St. Patrick's Day, more numbed than sorrowing.

Finally Mum arrived. "Oh, you are lucky," one of my classmates thoughtlessly exclaimed. *Lucky?*

Mum and Dad together with Liz and me in 1938. We didn't know it then, but our time together was coming to an end. Dad died in 1942, before we were reunited.

Liz and I were taken into a part of the convent reserved for the nuns and ushered into a parlour. Feeling shy and strange, I stared. Across the room stood a woman in a brown dress, her hair streaked with white. She looked frail and lonely.

Why, that's my Mum! I thought. Nothing like the mother who ran the house and our lives, whom I would never think of contradicting, of whom I was somewhat in awe. There was a moment of turmoil inside me, and then I realized, with a rush of love, that this new person was not just my mother — she was a friend. She would be a friend for life.

We hugged and kissed, and then Mum began to tell us, not all at once but over the next few days, and more in the years to come, what it had been like living with a man who was dying of leukemia. Dad had not been told how serious his illness was, for the specialist felt that if he knew, Dad might just "give up." So Mum had borne that secret alone for more than three years.

Mum also explained that I wouldn't be able to stay at school another year, as had been planned. Oxford was out of the question — there was no money anymore. Dad didn't even qualify for a pension — he was only forty-nine when he died. The best I could count on was a Carnegie scholarship to Edinburgh University, because Dad had been in the faculty of mathematics there.

Mum went home, looking very frail and lonely; we finished the school year and I sat the Senior Oxford Certificate, getting distinction in English and mathematics and earning an exemption from Matriculation and Responsions, which meant that I was free to go to any university in Britain without sitting the entrance exam. Not that it mattered now. There was no choice anymore.

It was a disappointment, but it was nothing like the loss of Dad. *If only there wasn't a war, we would have all been together at home, instead of being separated,* I thought. *Mum wouldn't have had to face it alone, and we would have seen Dad, perhaps even have had a chance to become friends and been part of the last farewell at his funeral. This miserable war!*

So, with the summer holidays, came the end of school for me. I couldn't really believe that Dad wasn't sitting in his familiar study, that we'd never see him again. *Why couldn't we have been there to say goodbye?* But life had to go on. In Britain one didn't make fusses. Pilots and sailors were dying. People were being bombed. Ours was just a very small personal loss.

I longed to join the navy. I had romantic dreams of being terribly brave in some unspecified situation. *Suppose the war ends while I am still too young to fight?* I thought.

Grudgingly I registered in an honours maths program at the university, but my heart wasn't in it. I got through my first year, and by then I was seventeen and a half — almost old enough. I volunteered, had interviews, medicals, filled in forms, and, finally, on my eighteenth birthday, November 3, 1943, I was given a train pass and told to report to Mill Hill in London. Finally I was old enough to fight!

In 1946 I was stationed on a Fleet Air Arm base in Belfast, Northern Ireland. I was one of a crew of meteorological observers, responsible for the hourly weather reports from Belfast, that, together with all the other reports from across the British Isles, made up the weather maps used by the Allied Command.

Monica Hughes, W.R.N.S. (Women's Royal Naval Service).

My favourite time was night watch, when I was alone in the weather room. Every hour I had to go outside to take readings and observe cloud conditions. The only lights were those coming from the big shipyards.

When the night was clear and the sky brilliant with stars, unspoiled by the glare of city lights, I used to stand outside, looking into space, and it was then that I got in touch with my father again and began to discover my future. He had introduced me to astronomy when I was twelve and had promised to take me to the Edinburgh Observatory. But the war had come, the Observatory was closed for the duration, and Dad was gone.

During those nights, as I gazed past war-torn earth at the tranquil vision of planets and stars, I began to dream — a dream that would persist all my life. My dream began with the question: What if we could travel in space? What if, like Jules Verne's adventurers in the science fiction stories I had loved to borrow from the Carnegie library in Edinburgh in the years before the war, we could travel to the moon? What if . . . ? The war was over and now there was hope.

MONICA HUGHES *left the navy and lived in Zimbabwe before settling in Canada in 1952. She went on asking, "What if?," becoming Canada's best-known, best-loved writer of science fiction for young people. She has also excelled as a writer of Young Adult historical fiction and contemporary novels. Monica won the Canada Council Award for Children's Literature twice in a row, in 1982 for* The Guardian of Isis *and 1983 for* Hunter in the Dark. *Numerous other awards include the Vicky Metcalf Award for a body of work. Her explorations constantly take new turns as youthful heroes pit themselves against inimical worlds, but always, in the end, "there is hope."*

JOY KOGAWA

AND

TIMOTHY NAKAYAMA

Far away from where I sit, halfway across this continent, halfway across the ocean, on an island, in a crib beside a window of a large, sunny house, is a tiny child.

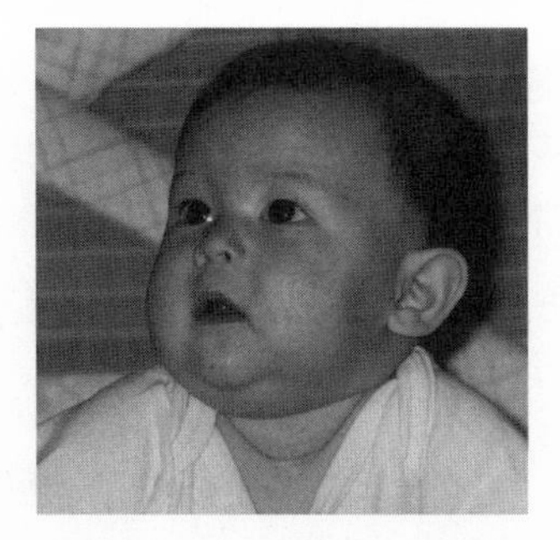

My daughter's perfect daughter, Anne Canute.

She is as perfect as anything I can imagine. I think about her all the time — my daughter's daughter, five months old.

Words are such clumsy things — like paws instead of hands. With these awkward scribblings, I cannot convey the sense of her, that first moment of waking and the wide-eyed babbling, one baby eyebrow lifted in glee. She's too young for fight or flight. She can barely roll over, front to back. How, without being maudlin, does one talk of babies and tenderness — an elemental tenderness? The tenderness rocks my daughter. It rocks the baby. I cannot describe the power of this and the tug.

A mysterious universe this is, that grants us life and breath, that brings us swimming through the warm red channels of birth. And here we find ourselves, flipping and flopping as we flounder along the tortuous paths of our lives, changing as we go, for good and for ill, becoming who we will be. In our efforts to connect, to disconnect, to reconnect, we are hardly aware of the chances and choices that beset us. Chaos and order chase each other round and round the mulberry bush, round and round our conundrums and the paradoxes of earthly life. Some of us will wend our way through it all with courage and gentleness. But others among us are so brutal and brutalized that the spark of humanity within is all but extinguished. We have heard of such people, hardly recognizable as human, for whom a baby is merely a toy to toss into the air and spear on the end of a bayonet. This is the kind of thing that happens thanks, in large part, to that human invention called war.

War.

A small word. Three letters. State-sanctioned murder. It's like the madness on the island of Dr. Moreau where animals are tortured and stitched and cobbled together to become pseudo-humans. In war, humans are ground to pieces to become killer machines.

My brother, Tim, and I were children, born and raised in Canada, when the insanity known as World War II broke out. Tim, who is now a retired Episcopalian priest, told me recently about an aspect of the war that I knew little about — the Battle of Okinawa.

Okinawa, the "Island of Peace" south of Japan, once had a king who outlawed violence. No swords, weapons, or soldiers. Napoleon was reported to have said, "A place with no weapons, no military? It must be heaven." It was.

Tim was in Okinawa in 1995 when the fiftieth anniversary of the Battle of Okinawa took place. Every single human being who died was remembered in the long, long reading of names — each small child, teenager, mother, teacher, farmer, even the foreign soldiers who had come to bring death — each person, friend, or foe who died in the battle was embraced in memory. A breathtaking act. The Gospel of Okinawa.

In 1945, on that idyllic tropical island, more than 236,000 people belonging to the world's most gentle, child-loving cultures died in the "typhoon of steel," died in the caves, died committing suicide jumping over the coral cliffs — grandparents with babies in their arms, sisters and brothers leaping hand in hand. It was the greatest number of non-combatant deaths to be recorded in any battle up to that time, more than the number killed by the two atomic bombs combined. Fragments of children's writings remain to tell us what happened.

Nothing Tim and I experienced in our Canadian childhood can begin to compare with that unthinkable tragedy. Our wartime stories were certainly about grave injustices and racism, and the internal scars we carry are real. "But you were allowed at least to live," some of our fellow citizens used to say to us, shrugging their shoulders. "If you were an enemy in Japan, or Germany, you'd have been killed."

We'd stare back silently, thinking, "But we weren't your enemies."

Our family lived in Vancouver, B.C., before the war. My brother was a young musical genius who wore glasses, and I was his pouty-mouthed kid sister who didn't talk or smile or charm anyone. I was relatively healthy, but Tim was not a strong child. He'd been born prematurely, weighing only a bit over four pounds at birth, and he fit in the palm of our father's hand. Dad used to tell us this, his outstretched hand cupped to show us how tiny his son had been. I pictured him as a denuded squirrel. He spent his newborn days in an incubator in Vancouver General Hospital.

One of my earliest, vaguest memories is of my brother in a cast. He tells me that was in 1937, two weeks before he turned six. I was two. We were living in our comfortable house in a pleasant area of Vancouver called Marpole, between Granville and Oak on 64th Avenue, not far from David Lloyd George School.

"What was that white cocoon you were in when you were a kid?" I asked him. "What was it all about?"

"Legge-Perthes disease." He spelled the name out. He had just started school but his right hip hurt and he limped. He doesn't limp anymore, but his right leg is slightly shorter and one shoulder just barely droops.

At first the doctors thought he had TB. A nightmare. The whole family was put through tests. Tuberculosis then was like AIDS today. A frightening, somehow shameful thing to hide. It was all too common among Asians in general and Japanese in particular.

But then they found out it wasn't TB and Tim wasn't going to infect everyone in sight, after all. He was stuck for five and a half months in a body case from the tip of his toes to the top of his neck — five and a half months as a little Egyptian mummy, buried in a stiff white tomb.

One day, the cast iron bars along his body cracked inside so the plaster had to be hacked away and as the new cast dried, nauseous fumes filled his nostrils. The mummy was crying to be let free. Another time he was in the Vancouver General Hospital in the children's ward, and he remembers the shock of nurses yelling at the children.

Not once in our long lives did Tim or I ever hear our parents shout in anger. On one occasion Dad showed Mama something he'd written and she didn't quite approve. She didn't come out and say anything. She just didn't give her approval. Dad took the paper — he was showing it to her in the kitchen — and he kind of snatched it up. I was startled by the aggression. Then he walked back to his desk. And that was it. That was a fight.

As a child I used to feel cursed for being flat-faced, black-haired, and Japanese, but later — much later — I knew better. Our parents were deeply sensitive and came from a child-centred culture. The community was a cocoon — a different one from Tim's — but a protective case nonetheless.

Tim was rescued from the world of yelling nurses when two Anglican missionaries, Father William Henry Gale and gentle Peggy Foster, visited him. The kindly priest and the whispery-voiced kindergarten teacher with the smiling eyes asked to have him transferred to an adult ward.

The day Tim came home, he was straddled front to back in his body cast — Humpty Dumpty in Father Gale's model "A" Ford. All through the rumbling drive home, he watched the key chain jiggling as it dangled from the ignition lock. He studied the timing lever on the steering column. The little boy who wanted a Meccano set more than anything else in the world remembered these mechanical details.

At home, Tim was Robert Louis Stevenson in "The Land of Counterpane," flat on his bed for months, ordering and controlling his wind-up world — a clock that ticked, a clock that didn't tick, pulleys and wheels and rubber-band gadgets.

The day finally came when the organizer was released from his cast. "Down to the armpits," Tim said, "then up to the knees; then around the hips.

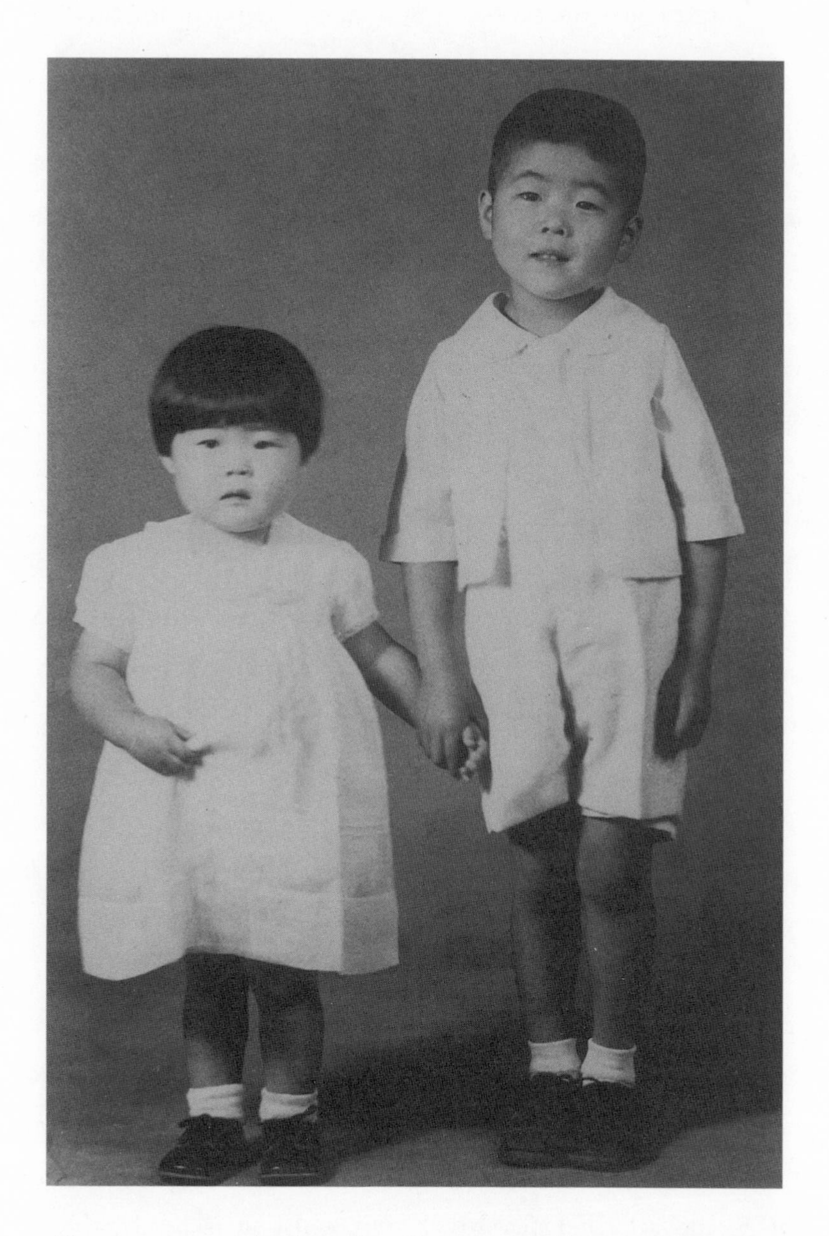

Tim was a young musical genius, and I was his pouty-mouthed kid sister who didn't talk or smile or charm anyone. Here we are in Vancouver, 1937, ages 2 and 6.

And finally I was out of the thing."

Like a toddler learning to walk, Tim had to start all over again, hobbling along on his little crutches, step-hop, step-hop, thick calluses forming on his piano-playing hands. But eventually, although he was never athletic, "my legs got going," Tim said.

His run was a kind of gallop. A bit of bravado in it. Life picked up where he'd left it and he was playing with the neighbourhood kids at last.

Our life in Marpole, Vancouver, before World War II was an ordinary Canadian story. We played hide-and-seek with the Steeves boys next door, we ran down to the corner store to buy a loaf of bread for a nickel, we attended the Gospel Hall nearby as well as our Anglican Church of the Ascension, a streetcar ride away in Kitsilano. But after Japan bombed Pearl Harbor, life for Canadians of Japanese descent was never the same again.

The day before Pearl Harbor was Saturday, December 6, 1941. Tim was visiting a classmate's home that morning with a couple of friends, and the father gave each boy some milk in the kitchen. Then on Monday morning, December 8, he was coming into the soccer field at the corner of the schoolyard, and his classmate came over to him and sneered, "You dirty yellow Jap." It stopped him cold. Tiny Tim, finally healthy enough to play soccer, "got it" immediately and felt sick in the pit of his stomach. Friendship on Saturday and a dirty yellow Jap on Monday. And in between was Sunday, December 7. Pearl Harbor.

Everything was still the same for Tim that Sunday before we got to church in Kitsilano — our beautiful church with the smooth light oak everywhere. People loved the place. We'd built it completely on our own without a penny of outside help. That church at Third and Pine, our other church on Cordova farther downtown, our house in Marpole, the hospital, stores, rooming houses, farms, fishing villages — all our visible heritage disappeared forever in the bureaucratic whirlwind that followed Pearl Harbor. Church and State joined unholy hands together in a money-driven dance, and our dear Church of the Ascension was sold. Not a word to us. Not a penny to the community. At some point years later it became a furniture factory. Then it was demolished and a pharmaceutical company was built. The place of prayer became a place of pills.

Back on that fateful day, Sunday, December 7, 1941, I was sitting in the pews snuggled up to Mama in her coat trimmed with fur, her little hat with the pheasant feather angled jauntily to the side. Tim in his wire-rimmed glasses, his grey tweed jacket, short pants, and knee socks listened, puzzling as the adults whispered discreetly in the hush before worship. After the service there was no visible panic, but serious faces looked down at the floor. Dad (our father, the priest in charge) was talking with some of the leaders about holding a meeting to try to make sense of the situation. There was a kind of charged intensity in the murmuring. That evening, about a dozen people came to our house in Marpole and huddled around the big radio in the living room. Tim was sent to bed early. That was odd. He knew something was badly wrong. With his ear to the closed door, he heard the name "Cordell Hull." Who, he wondered, was Cordell Hull? Years later, he learned that he was the U.S. Secretary of State, conducting talks with government officials of Japan. Then he heard someone say, "It will be at least twenty-five years from now before the truth is known."

On the phone I asked him, "The truth? About the bombing of Pearl Harbor?"

"I guess the point is," Tim said, "that any war report hides as many truths as it reveals. As they say, 'truth is the first casualty of war.'"

"Well, here in Canada, we were Canadian kids, far from the scene of the war . . ."

"But directly affected," Tim said. "Especially at school."

In 1941, we were both attending David Lloyd George Public School. Tim was an excellent student all around, but he was outstanding in music. The words were written in the teacher's neat handwriting on his report card that

Mama and Dad looked at solemnly. "Timothy is outstanding in music." They made no comment about this, neither congratulating him nor applauding. It was a simple fact. He was a born musician and the school conductor. He was also a boy soprano, chosen to go to the school in Kerrisdale to be part of the prestigious Vancouver Boys' Choir.

The boys were in furious competition with the Elgar Choir and were practising incessantly. And after one vigorous and satisfying session, one of the teachers — it was either the conductor or the pianist — gave a pep talk. The choir was in top form. They had to win. Every musical bone in Tim's body was as keen as a tuning fork and he was charged with urgency.

At that point of exhilaration and determination, a dark curtain fell. It was as if Tim was speeding with his team in a race through the rapids when he was tossed overboard. He had to report that he couldn't attend the competition. Japanese Canadians were under a curfew and couldn't go out at night.

The teachers, saddened, glanced at each other and shook their heads. Mama and Dad said, "*Shi-kata-ga-nai*," meaning, "There's nothing we can do." Literally, "No framework into which the matter can fit, therefore no way to resolve the problem."

For my part, all I knew was that something was wrong and dangerous in the world. It had something to do with airplanes. In school there was an air raid drill. A deafening alarm clanged. The teacher lifted her hand and we stood quickly beside our desks, turned and filed out row by row, into the hall and out to the schoolyard, scattering to the hedges and ditches. "Like this?" I asked Miss Brushkey as I crouched in a gap of the hedges. She nodded. "Yes, that's a good place."

At nights, there were eerie blackouts from time to time. No streetlights. Dad painted the light bulbs with blue-black ink. Mama cut and seamed heavy opaque blankets to cover the windows. The strange solemn activity was carried on in an intense hush, the hands urgent in the new darkness. Outside was the occasional ominous drone of planes. For me, the stillness already within was deepened in the blackouts and spread through my life. My silent, unsmiling childhood was suffused with a need not to intrude, not to get in the way.

One day, I was helping Mama hanging clothes on the line. I held up the wooden pegs one by one. We both saw Tim galloping in his lopsided way, down the back alley, fumbling at the latch of the gate, then across the backyard, rushing into the house through the playroom. His glasses were missing. Mama took a wooden peg out of her mouth. She said nothing. Neither did I. We followed him in and she took the glasses that were twisted in his fist, fixed them with white adhesive bandage tape. They flopped crookedly on his face and he shoved them back onto his stubby Japanese nose. Tim developed a nervous tic around this time.

War is not just state-sanctioned killing. It's state-sanctioned racism. It releases demons. And out they come, jumping into human skins — into little boys in soccer fields, into little girls who sneer. Tim and I were cast into a whole new virulent disease, the kind that attacks the soul, the kind we don't have microscopes for. We may not see the bacteria, but we hear the words. Sticks and stones may break our bones, but names, contrary to the childhood chant, can hurt us more.

Thankfully, although words do harm us, words also heal. Words of truth guide us, words create enchantment, kind words make us well.

Tim and I both became word gatherers. I gathered stories to escape. He gathered words for clues. Like babes lost in the woods, Tim and I looked for the pebbles and a pathway home. His set of words made no sense to me: *"Alien Registration, Consigning of chattels and real estate for safekeeping for the duration of the war."*

"And then I heard there was something called a 'weight limit of 150 pounds,'" Tim said, "and I discovered that it referred to train baggage per person to take to a 'relocation camp' and people were saying, 'Bring only what you need for camp.'"

One day Dad took Tim to visit the exhibition grounds at Hastings

Park. Inside the horticultural barns, colourful blankets hung as partitions around the beds that were the new homes for the Japanese Canadians who had been rounded up as enemies from up and down the B.C. coast. Outside the wire fence, people were buying and reading the *Vancouver Province.* Some adults were saying that the *Province* was more fair than the other paper about the "evacuation" and "relocation" that was authorized by an Order in Council of Prime Minister William Lyon Mackenzie King. "What an imposing mouthful of a name that seemed to me when I was ten years old," Tim said.

And suddenly in the middle of all that language, we were gone — disappeared by bureaucratic decree onto a soot-belching, coal-eating hulk of a train. The smoke came pouring into the open windows as we wound through the tunnels of the Coquihalla Pass. We felt the gritty texture and spit the soot out of our mouths — an acrid taste. Tim, inclined to allergies and more delicate than I, blew his nose, and tears streamed down his face. But out of the tunnels, the scenery was spectacular. A never-ending army of tall evergreens flit past the windows. Rivers. Waterfalls. Snow patches. Mountain tops. Deep chasms. After our train journey we were on a bus from Nelson for fifty-one winding miles, and the bus driver was announcing our destination as "Slow-cn."

Slocan was a spindly old ghost town. Drab grey abandoned hotels leaned into each other on the short main street. But the lake was as clear and crisp as a spring morning, and the air of the mountains moved through us with the pure healing scent of evergreens.

Tim was told the story of how Slocan got its name one day when he was out on a barge on the lake. On the steep rock faces along the western shore he saw Indian picture writing and learned that the Indians who discovered the valley used to say, "If you go slow, you can go." That is, the mountains were so high, the rock faces so steep, the forest so dense, you could get lost. But if you went slowly, without panicking, down the mountain to the river or lake, you would find your way. *Slow-can-go.* The local people knew how to pronounce the name: *Slow-can,* not *Slow-cn.*

When we first arrived, we didn't have enough food. All that first morning, Mama, Tim, and I waddled through the forest on our haunches, like three ducks, picking dandelion leaves. Then back home at our newspaper-lined hut, Mama burnt sticks, making ashes, then ash water, in which she soaked the leaves overnight to get the bitterness out of them.

Tim and I both have happy memories of Slocan — hiking up the mountains, picking berries in lard tins, gathering mushrooms — light, floppy, fragrant mushrooms, dark brown and soft as a dog's ears, growing on mossy fallen trees deep in the heart of the mountain away from the paths. In early spring a million fiddleheads poked primly out of the forest floor. Snap. And into the bucket.

Eventually there were also chickens — a hapless huddle of cluck-clucking white Leghorns and Rhode Island Reds, looking alarmed all the day long as they scratched the soil raw in the chicken yard. And the babies! I'd watch the eggs under the brooding hens cracking open a tiny peck at a time until out would flop a wet little skeleton of a thing barely alive. In no time it would dry out into a cheeping yellow fluffball. Most of the eggs were shared with others. In the morning, I'd go into the smelly chicken coop and search the straw nests on the ledges, picking up the sometimes warm eggs, gently so as not to break them.

The big rooster chased the younger smaller roosters, all their red waggly chin bits trembling as they jumped and squawked or strutted about. Occasionally a young rooster would be killed, held upside down by its feet, its tiny head flopped on the chopping block.

I never got used to that. I'd sit on the stoop of the outhouse, watching, praying. Whack! The axe was on the block in one brutal blow and the chicken released to leap flapping and headless over the garden. I clutched my knees. Dear God, is it over? Is the suffering over? Only the chicken knew and it couldn't tell me. A terrible silence.

I have been acquainted with silence all my life — the silence of the people who suffered but did not complain. The silence of the community. We generally did not talk about the painful experiences — the theft of our properties, countless keepsakes and treasures entrusted to the custodian for "safekeeping," ruthlessly auctioned off, the loss of schooling, the breakup of families, the calculated destruction of all community in the dispersal across the country.

There are thousands of stories. Hundreds and thousands of stories of hardship and grief, hopes and dreams and life-savings lost. Little Japanese Canadian kids lived in the rows and rows of huts in Bayfarm or Lemon Creek, Popoff, Sandon, Tashme or New Denver, Rosebery or Kaslo — crowded together, two families each in tiny shared cabins, one room per family, one stove, without water, without plumbing. They weren't as lucky as we were.

None of us attended school for the first year and a half in Slocan. But eventually Pine Crescent school was built in Bayfarm. In the next year and a half, Tim went from grade five to grade seven and I covered grades two to four. High-school graduates taught us. Others helped. A beautician, Mrs. Homma, taught hygiene. Sam Matsumoto, a ship builder, taught drafting and carpentry. Our home became the school's publishing house with shoe polish "ink" in Dad's duplicating machine.

Anglican women missionaries, some who came from out of retirement, taught high school and kindergarten. Hattie Horobin, Gertie Shore, Elsie Heaps, Peggy Foster, Eleanor Hawkins, Alice Cox, Grace Tucker, Nora Bowman — this stalwart army of the faithful stood by the castaway Canadians.

Grace Tucker stood by the castaway Canadians.

Grace Tucker, at 96, is the last of the group left, now living in a retirement home in Richmond, B.C. She's a brilliant and witty woman. I talked with her not too long ago and asked her what she thought of the "blessing in disguise" theory. Many people used to say that what happened to us was a blessing in disguise because after the war, we were dispersed across the whole country and assimilated. And she said, "Oh no, Joy, I never thought any of it was a blessing."

I agreed with her. To say it was a "blessing," exonerates the oppressor, for one thing. "But people do try to make the best of things," I said. "I mean, for example, when we think about Slocan, we like to remember the happy times, swimming, climbing the mountains. We bury our negative memories — the thousand little traumas of racism that were our daily diet. Being despised. Being snubbed by white Canadians. Being portrayed in newspapers as ugly, as unwanted, as deceitful, as somehow sub-human."

Tim was in a cast for five and a half months, but the community took forty years to emerge and address the painful truths. There's a word psychologists use. *Denial.* Without our being aware of it, one silken memory at a time had bubbled up to cocoon us in happy stories, pleasant half-truths. But the time came when we were compelled, both from inside pressures and outside forces, to acknowledge the fuller reality, to look at our buried traumas and tragedies, and to work to prevent a reoccurrence of the events for others. The time of readiness was like a morning in spring. Icicles had begun to melt. People had begun to hear. What's important was that we recognized that a turning point had come.

My brother and I were in different countries, he in the United States and I in Canada, during the communities' struggle for redress. In both countries, loyal American and Canadian citizens of Japanese ancestry were seeking acknowledgement of the injustices. And in both countries, we met resistance from within the communities and from without. Some people were not ready to come out of their cocoons.

In Canada, twenty-one thousand of us along the B.C. coast had been stripped of our rights and properties. Even after the war, we were not allowed to return. Our homes were sold to others, our farms in the Fraser Valley were handed over to war veterans, some of us were exiled to Japan, and the rest of us were dispersed across the country, a few here, some there, never to become a geographic community again.

Tim and me with our parents in Lethbridge, Alberta

Many among us resisted the struggle for redress — not wanting to "rock the boat," fearful of a backlash. We had finally achieved invisibility of a sort. And acceptance.

And so, patiently, over the years, the leaders of the redress movement carried the energy forward bit by bit, educating people, reaching out, making a path through the forest. And finally on September 22, 1988, the government of Canada officially acknowledged the injustices.

We had come to a particular springtime moment. The temperature was right, the waiting time was over, and we broke through the big white cast that had kept us silenced — down to the armpits; up to the knees; then around the hips. And finally we were out of the thing — out of the prison of injustice, out of years of being second-class citizens, out into the clear light of a new Canadian day. If we had missed that breakthrough moment, we might have ended up just another casualty of history, a mummified, dried-up chrysalis, a victim of racism forever. But thanks to the courage and tenacity of the people, thanks to the warmth and support of thousands of fellow citizens, we were able to break through the walls of denial together.

My new little grandchild, barely out of one womb, has many walls still ahead of her, more cocoons from which to emerge, more worlds to discover and troubles to overcome. She is too young to fight in wars, but not too young to fight her way along the path of her earthly life. Soon she will be fighting the forces of gravity to stand upright on her two pudgy legs. I pray that her journey will be as blessed and freeing and as full of joy and truth as mine has been thus far.

JOY KOGAWA *became an award-winning author and social activist. She studied education, music, and theology, holds four honorary doctorates, and is a member of the Order of Canada. Joy first established her literary reputation as a poet, but her novel* Obasan *(1981) touched the hearts of Canadians everywhere; it was arguably the single most important influence on the national conscience, enabling readers to enter the lives of 20,000 people who had been dispossessed of their property and their country. In the latter 1990s, Joy has focused on improving the lives of poor people through the Toronto Dollar.*

TIMOTHY NAKAYAMA *became an Episcopal priest, serving mostly in the United States, and now, in active semi-retirement, in Japan. Tim retained an interest in music, but did not become a musician. By the time his father arranged for a piano and lessons in Slocan, a crucial "year or two" had vanished. Tim was only ten years old, however, when he began to feel called to ordained ministry. As a farewell after twenty-five years in Seattle, the city declared a "Timothy Nakayama Day."*

CLAIRE MACKAY

1939 May 21: The King and Queen are coming!

Tomorrow they drive right up Parkside Drive where we live. Uncle Bill laughed when he heard about it. He and Ruby — who is supposed to be his wife but she doesn't have a wedding ring — live on the second floor now. I guess they pay some rent, because Mom says every little bit helps. But I don't think he should laugh at the King. The King can't help being King — his big brother wouldn't take the job. Big brothers always try to get out of work. I know. Anyway, Uncle Bill says the reason the King and Queen have come is to get everybody stirred up about going to war. And to get rid of all the men who don't have good jobs. Like Dad, I guess. But the most important thing is that we can make money. Dad says people will pay just to sit on our front lawn.

So Grant and I cleaned up the lawn and swept the sidewalk and the steps and the verandah. Big brothers don't like work but they do like money and Mom said she'd pay our way to the show next week. On THE BIG DAY 72 people showed up. Uncle Bill got some chairs from the union hall, and people who had chairs paid 75 cents and people who didn't sat on the bare grass and paid 50 cents. Dad said they had more money than brains. We collected the money in a tobacco tin before the parade started. Which was a good idea, because the whole thing was a big gyp. It was cold out and everybody had to wear sweaters, to start with. And it wasn't a real parade, with bands and soldiers and clowns. First a couple of motorcycles came up from Sunnyside. Andy, our dog, barked like mad — he hates motorcycles. Then a car and then nothing for a minute and then another car with some men in top hats and then nothing and then a long car without a top went by at about sixty miles an hour. We saw two little toy people, like dolls, in the back seat, with their hands lifted up. One doll had a big hat. People were cheering. I didn't cheer. Grant said it wasn't the King and Queen at all, just two statues of them, like the models in Eaton's windows. That's all I can say about it. BUT — we made THIRTY-EIGHT DOLLARS AND FIFTY CENTS.

The King and Queen looked like two little toy people, like dolls, in the back seat, with their hands lifted up.

June 4: At last we got to go to the show, the Revue on Roncesvalles. At night! First time we've gone to a show at night. It cost twelve cents. We almost didn't get to go, because of my dumb brother. Auntie Audrey gave him a magnifying glass and he went around burning things with it. He set his own shoelaces on fire, and now he has to have butcher string in his shoes until we can buy new shoelaces. Mom said she was EXASPERATED! (I had to look that up in the big dictionary. It means "annoyed extremely.") But she let us go. We saw *The Four Feathers.* All about soldiers in Africa, and some of them think one guy, Harry, is a coward so they send him a white feather. (That means coward.) It isn't true, but he has to prove it by saving his friends. He pretends he's an Arab slave and gets branded on his forehead. That was when Grant ran to the bathroom as usual. When he saw the witch in *Snow White*, he hid under the seat! (I don't mean the toilet seat, ha-ha!)

Mom with me and Grant in 1939, just before the war.

September 9: Uncle Bill and Ruby went to Blairmore in Alberta to organize the coal miners so the flat is empty. Mom says it's hard to make ends meat. We hardly ever have meat anyway. Today the *Star* had big black headlines, saying "WAR DECLARED." Our teacher Miss Warren looked sad all day. Somebody said her boyfriend was killed in the Great War. I looked it up in the *Book of Knowledge* and it was way back in 1914. She must be old! Dad says it's a stupid war, and it's really all about money.

October 15: Today is Mom and Dad's wedding day. They have been married twelve years. They went dancing at the Palais Royale. Auntie Audrey came to look after us. She is showing me how to knit wristlets to keep the sailors' wrists warm.

November 23: I am friends with a boy two doors up. His name is Benny. I'm getting sick of Dougie. He's okay, but he's always, ALWAYS hanging around. He knocks on the back door at 6:30 in the morning! And he keeps giving me dumb stuff. A hankie, with a pink S on it. A chestnut he scratched a heart on. A little blue bottle of Evening in Paris perfume, mostly all gone. Probably stole it from his mother. Last week he gave me a squashed baloney sandwich! Besides his hair sticks up all over and he has so many freckles he looks like a giant carrot. Benny doesn't have a single freckle. Anywhere. I asked him. (He said he'd prove it if I wanted. Ha-ha!)

November 27: Baloney is not spelled baloney. I looked it up. It is spelled bologna, from a city in Italy. When I told Dad, he laughed and said it's from all the stuff they sweep up off the floor at Canada Packers out in the Junction. Sometimes Dad is disgusting.

1940

February 1: I'll be ten this year. It sounds a lot older than nine. I'm still friends with Benny. He collects stuff, like me. He has a bunch of fish (alive) in a tank, and some butterflies (dead) stuck on beaverboard with coloured pins, and an album of Polish stamps (his grandparents live there), and a drawer full of different kinds of stones. I have Canadian stamps, mostly King George, but one Queen Victoria and two King Edward (the first one, not the one who didn't want the job), some British Empire ones, four coins from Spain, thirteen Action Comics, and seven cat's-eye marbles. I've just started to save bubblegum cards. I have eleven. I'm also saving bubblegum because there's a rumour that they won't make any more until after the war. They need the rubber in it to make tires. (I was saving chewed bubblegum, too, under my window sill, but Mom found it and made me pick it off and throw it away. I had it all lined up in order, too. Some of it was still pretty good.)

February 19: Today is Nana Arland's birthday. She lives on St. Mary's Street now, with my Auntie Audrey, and she has roomers. (That's the other spelling for rumours.) We went to her house for supper. We don't know where Grandpa is. Mom doesn't talk about him. He went to Russia when I was two. Before he went he painted the living-room floor red and put a yellow hammer and sickle in the corner, like the USSR flag.

My Nana Arland (middle) with her daughters, my mother and Aunt Audrey to her right. We don't know where Grandpa is.

February 20: I HATE that Shirley up the street! She is so M-E-A-N! Benny and I were skating on Grenadier Pond — I can't skate very well, they are old skates and the ankles are all cracked and so are mine after I skate — anyway we were having a nice time and then Shirley and Eleanor (who steals stuff from Kresge's, I know because she wanted me to do it, too, or I couldn't be in their stupid gang, and who cares anyway?) came over and started saying bad stuff about Benny and me, that we did things in the bushes, and stuff like that. I got so mad I ran right up to Shirley and pushed her down. She's such a sissy she started to bawl. Then Eleanor said stuff to Benny about that little cap on his head and called him a dirty, greedy Jew, and they ran away, yelling "Three fingers for the Jew! You killed Christ!" Benny looked sort of sick. The whole day was ruined and we went back to his house. He didn't want to tell, so I did. Then his mom started to cry. And she hugged Benny and cried and rocked back and forth and cried. I got out of there.

February 22: I asked Benny about his hat. He said it's a yarmulke (he spelled it for me — he's a good speller, like me), and Jewish men and boys wear it. Then I asked him about killing Christ. He said Christ was a Jew and it was really the Romans who killed him, but lots of people don't like Jews so they made up that story. He said Adolf Hitler, who runs Germany and started the war, hates the Jews, too. I said we should start calling Eleanor and Shirley Adolf, and he laughed. At last. I asked him why his mother cried and he said his grandparents had their store burnt down, and they might be put in jail for being Jewish, and his mother was worried. Maybe I will give him my Queen Victoria stamp.

February 25: It's cold. Outside and inside. Mom said it's been below zero every day since Christmas. We haven't got any coal for the furnace so on Saturday we went to Grandpa Bacchus's and chopped up old pianos in his backyard. He got them from working for Heintzman's. They were fun to wreck. But now the wood's all gone, even for the jacket heater. I had to wear my coat to bed and my mitts to read. Right now I'm reading *Beautiful Joe.* It's sad. I love it.

February 28: One good thing happened today — we had our telephone cut off. I hate telephones. They ring when I'm reading. When I grow up I am never EVER going to have a telephone. It's still cold, but it was really warm for about an hour last night. Mom nearly burnt the house down. She was so sick of being cold she threw a can of Domestic Shortening into the furnace. (I wonder if there is Lengthening, too?) Heat came out of the registers like a big wind. Grant said he saw flames, what a liar! Dad said we could have fried an egg — if we had an egg — on the furnace pipes. Alan, the man who comes to run the printing machine in the back bedroom, got all upset. There are huge stacks of paper there for the leaflets and papers. And a pile of pamphlets by Tim Buck (he's the leader of the Communist Party) and some other guys. Grant and I aren't supposed to tell anybody about that. Alan gets upset easy. He's kind of strange — he got wounded in the leg over in Spain fighting Franco. He says that the Mounties and the police are spying on us, and I did see somebody sitting in The Easy Tree in the park across the street. So the next time I saw Benny I said we might go to jail, too, just like his grandparents. He was impressed.

April 15: Things are mixed up. We had to move from Parkside. The bailiff came and gave us five days to get the fifty dollars we owed for rent. Mom said it might as well be fifty million dollars. So they took most of our furniture except for the beds, the kitchen table, and four chairs. They even took the old moth-eaten chesterfield, which I think Mom is glad about. It is mohair. When I was small, Dad told me that the chesterfield was made from the fur of a thousand moes, which were tiny squirrels in Australia. Funny Dad. We left at the end of March in a big hurry. When I went to say goodbye to Benny, he ran into his house, then ran back out and gave me a little gold box. He started to bawl, and so did I. Inside the box was a gold chain with a six-pointed star on it. (It is a Star of David, special to Jewish people.) I gave him my Queen Victoria stamp . . . Anyway, now we're living on Collier Street, in a little second-floor flat. We don't have a telephone, hurray! On the first floor are Mr. and Mrs. Simpson and two big boys Fred and Bill. All of them fight and yell at each other all the time. Except for old Mrs. Simpson, the grandmother on the third floor. She mostly yells at the furniture. Especially the chamberpot.

May 21: Germany is bombing England every night, and some kids are going to be sent over here to get away from it. Grant and I are collecting coloured pictures of airplanes from the *Star Weekly* rotogravure section. Bill and Fred are helping us build little model planes out of balsa wood. So far we have two Spitfires, a Hurricane, a Mosquito bomber, two Messerschmitts, and a Stuka. They have tiny propellers and tiny canopies, with tiny pilots underneath them, and all the proper markings stuck on. We hang them from our ceiling with thread, and they sway with every passing breath. (I stole that from a book.)

Grant and I collected pictures of airplanes from the *Star Weekly* and made little model planes

June 25: Last night was good and bad. Dad went to work (he has a job three nights a week for a couple of hours, 20 cents an hour), and Mom and Grant and I went down to Duke Street to help give food to the unemployed. We stayed to play Chinese Checkers and poker with them. Grant won two cents and then lost them. He said he's never going back. We were having fun and we didn't get home till 12:30. Dad was there and, boy, he was upset! We got sent to bed, but you can hear everything in this place, and I heard my Dad crying! He thought Mom had gone away with us and wasn't coming back because we didn't have any money and he didn't have a decent job. Then Mom started to cry and said she was scared he'd have to go in the army. So I cried, just a little. (I always cry when my mom cries.) I bet Grant did, too.

July 30: Tim Buck has disappeared. Alan has disappeared. So has Lionel Edwards (a really good friend of Mom and Dad and Nana). He was in the Spanish War, too, and he is handsome, even though a bullet dented his forehead. Mom says they went underground. Or maybe they're in jail. People can be kept in jail just for disagreeing with the government. A lot of Italian people had their store windows smashed, now that Italy has joined Hitler, and some were put in jail. That's not fair. Dad says we're getting like Nazi Germany. The Red Squad — that's a bunch of Toronto cops — are raiding people's houses. They almost raided Nana's. Auntie Audrey ran home from selling the *Tribune* and said a cop on a horse had chased her. So Nana gathered up all the books by Karl Marx and Lenin and Bernard Shaw and all the papers and pamphlets by Tim Buck and Becky Buhay and Annie Buller and threw them in the furnace. In July! Her roomers got awful hot, and they couldn't understand why Annie Arland had the furnace on! . . . Bill and Fred joined the army, and Mr. Simpson joined, too. Mom made a joke — she does that about once a year — and said, "Well, the way they fight, the war should be over in a week!"

September 20: We moved again, across the street to 146. It's a real house. The rent is $25 a month. Uncle Doug and Aunt Isobel live on our second floor. Uncle Doug has a good job with Aikenhead's Hardware. (He has flat feet so the Army didn't want him.) And guess what? Dad has a steady job, too!! Yippee! He's figuring out all the war tax and doing payrolls for war workers. I go to Rosedale School now, where all the rich kids go. And I'm in grade five! I skipped grade four and I'm glad. I won't have scary old Miss Millar. Her eyes are black and glittery. (I bet Grant would hide under his seat!) We have six refugee kids and they're rich, too. Most of the poor kids in England didn't get a chance to come. One girl has a beautiful-sounding name, Gillian Brocklebank. Some of the boys are a bit stuck-up, and they dress funny — grey short pants, grey V-neck sweaters, and ties! And they are all VERY smart, especially Paul C.

1941

January 11: We had a Christmas tree even though it cost 60 cents. Mom and Dad gave me a microscope! Grant and I gave Dad a flat fifty of Sweet Caporals and Mom some new Tangee lipstick and Cutex nail polish. She is secretary of Ward 6 Housewives Consumers Association and goes to meetings a lot. I hope Dad smokes fast. Then he'll go back to roll-your-owns, and I can earn some money. He has a little roller that does one cigarette at a time and he gives me 1 cent for every ten cigarettes I make. Mom and I went out every night before the January elections delivering leaflets. Mom said we had to be silent and invisible. I felt like Robin Hood or the Scarlet Pimpernel (which I just finished reading). If we got caught by the police, we'd be in trouble . . . I was right about that Paul. He stood first and I stood second in November; in December I was first and he was second. If only he wasn't so snooty about it . . . Maybe he's just shy, like me . . .

May 29: Dr. Lowrie was arrested! Our doctor, our good, wonderful doctor, who took care of all of us for nothing when we were poor, was arrested! Nobody can believe it! He hasn't done anything wrong but they know he's friends with people in the Party. He came when I had that terrible whooping cough, and when I split my head open on the ice, and when Grant had scarlet fever! They took him away from his office on Humewood in handcuffs! He is in a camp in Petawawa, and Mom says he has to wear a shirt with a big yellow circle on it. Dad said, "Easier for the guards to shoot him in the back!" I felt sick until Dad said he was joking. But is he? Anyway, it was in the *Toronto Daily Star* and the *Globe and Mail*. Not the *Telegram* though, which Dad calls a fascist rag. We're scared he might get shot at, or beaten up, like Tim Buck was when I was little. I hate the people who did this. I hate the government. I hate the Red Squad. They park at the end of our street nearly every day, watching. We are handing out petitions that say, "Free Dr. Lowrie!" Maybe we should give one to the cops . . .

August 24: Hitler attacked Russia. Now everybody loves Russia and Communists. They are called "our brave allies." What a joke! There was a big party at our house to celebrate. Boxes of beer were piled up to the ceiling, and everybody sang "Keep the Red Flag Flying," and "Long Live Our Soviet Motherland," and all the union songs. Also, "You Are My Sunshine" and "Sweet Violets," about a hundred verses. Some were funny. Art Celsie brought his guitar and his dad played concertina. Susie (not her real name — she is a "parlour pink" from the rich Maclean family) and Joe (not his real name either) necked like mad in the back hall, and Big Jim McCarthy, who is married to Lionel Edwards's sister, fell off the back verandah. I wonder what the cops thought . . . And I got a job! Grant got it for me, really. He's a pretty good brother sometimes. He was working at Yorkville Library but got a better job bringing home peoples' groceries from the Dominion store at Asquith and Yonge. He told the librarian I could do the job easily. And I got it! I work Saturdays in the Children's Section. I love it! The pay is 10 cents an hour. I'm going to read absolutely every book!

November 10: Our grade six teacher is Miss Lupton. She told Mom that my work was "splendid." She looks like a pin-up girl, and the boys stare at her chest all the time. I stood first again and Paul was second. Grant only got 49 in geography, so he couldn't listen to *The Lone Ranger* for a week. (I felt sorry for him so I turned the radio up if Mom wasn't around.) The Germans are trying to capture Moscow, but so far they haven't. We all went down to Maple Leaf Gardens last month for an Aid the Soviets meeting. Dorise Neilsen, a member of Parliament, spoke about the bravery of the Russians. Lots of big shots from business and government were there. I wonder if the Mounties know.

1942

February 14: Boy, a lot has happened! Guess who I got a valentine from? Yep. Paul! He stuck it in my desk during recess. Signed "P.C., with admiration." I looked at it, then I looked at him, and I could feel myself blush, darn it! He sort of saluted and smiled a bit. At least he's stopped wearing a tie. I also got one from Bobby Binks down the street. His brother Billy is in the air force . . . The Germans were turned back from Moscow. Japan bombed Honolulu on December 7, so the United States is finally in the war. About time. There's a Japanese family two doors down, and I know the kids Mary and Frank. Somebody threw fresh horse manure at their front door, and I saw their tiny mother come out and wash it off and hurry back inside without looking at anybody, as if she was ashamed. The person who threw it should be ashamed. God! Why are people so mean? The only thing I have against them is that Frank kicked our dog once . . . I had lots of time to read in January because I was sick for three whole weeks, with congestion in my lung. Mom put about ten mustard plasters on my chest. I read *Gone with the Wind* in three days, and Jack London's *White Fang*, *The Call of the Wild*, and *The Iron Heel*, which is all about socialism defeating fascism, and the world being at peace. And *Doctor Fu Manchu* and all of Emile Gaboriau's detective stories. Grant was sick, too, with fever and bad tonsils . . . Guess what? Ted Schofield asked me to go to the show at the York. *I Wanted Wings* is on, with Veronica Lake. (I'm trying to get my hair to look like hers.) I said okay. He's fifteen! He's very nice-looking but he scares me a bit. His dad's away in the navy . . .

May 24: Firecracker Day. Our gang, The Skulls Victory Gang (Ray, Fred, Ewan, Jackie, Grant, and me — we collect newspapers and tinfoil for the war effort) went down to Rosedale ravine to set off our stuff. We aimed a skyrocket at crabby old Mrs. True's back verandah. Put one toe on her lawn and she yells at you. She hates us and we hate her right back! (Hating is fun sometimes.) Anyway, it hit her fence instead. Jackie was kind of quiet because his big brother George is missing. He's a gunner in a bomber.

Some of the 1941 Skulls Victory Gang members: Fred, Grant, Ray, Ewan, David (not in the gang), and me.

August 15: Forgot to say Dr. Lowrie is out of prison at last. He was at a huge rally at Maple Leaf Gardens — 11,000 people showed up! Paul Robeson was there, in person! He sang "Ol' Man River" and "The Internationale." Everybody joined in for the second verse, "No more tradition's chains shall bind us/ Arise, ye slaves; no more in thrall/ The earth shall rise on new foundations/ We have been naught, we shall be all." I cried, and I wasn't the only one. His voice goes so low you can't hear it. You feel it instead, as if you swallowed some thunder. Afterwards we signed petitions to lift the ban on the Communist Party and to free all the political prisoners. Dr. Lowrie looked white and skinny. Mom said they put him in a cell by himself for a long time, until he got sick and nearly died. That is so cruel!

October 2: I am in grade eight! I was in grade seven for a week and then the principal asked Mom about putting me ahead, and she said okay. I'm a little scared though — everybody is bigger and older. Some are fourteen and one boy is fifteen, and I'm still just eleven. It's easy so far, but some of the girls are mean. They talk about lipstick and Kotex and brassieres and riding lessons and going skiing, and when I try to get near them they laugh and say, "Be quiet, here comes Claire, the ignorant child!" I know things they can't even imagine, and I bet I beat them all. Except for Paul. I thought I'd leave him behind in grade seven but he skipped, too. I'm kind of glad . . .

October 6: Tim Buck surrendered! The *Daily Star* had a big picture of him walking into Mountie headquarters with a smile on his face. It was funny, really. The cops had hunted him all over the place for three years, without any luck. Tim gave himself up because he says Canada needs unity in the struggle, and he wants all anti-fascists to join forces and defeat the Axis. Stalingrad is still holding out — that's four months now, with many dead and many starving. They are so brave . . . Had to answer the phone. (Yes, we have a phone now, Princess 3667.) It was Ted. Show. Saturday, Uptown. John Garfield (EXTREMELY HANDSOME!) in *Dangerously They Live.* Do I really like Ted? There's something mean about him . . .

November 15: He's mean all right! What a skunk! He stood me up! Said he forgot! Then grinned at me, like a little kid who swiped a cookie. This isn't the first time either . . . Jackie's brother was killed. The telegram came last week. The first death on our block. Jackie goes around looking sad and important. Everybody is being nice to him, even the girls who always tease him for being fat. It might be interesting to have a dead brother.

November 27: I failed a Problems Test. I got 29 out of 60. I've never failed in my whole life. I cried in the cloakroom after school, and our teacher, Mr. Newton, found me there. He was very nice, said not to worry about one test, and I felt a little better. (He told Mom I have "rare ability," and that I should go to university. Not much chance of that . . .) Tim Buck and the other leaders got out of the Don Jail and we had another huge meeting at the Gardens. Guess who sat right beside Tim? Mitch Hepburn (the Liberal Premier of Ontario) and some bigshot Tory! It's enough to make you sick! They helped put him in prison ten years ago, and Hepburn hates unions. Auntie Audrey told me he hired a gang of goons to beat up the strikers at General Motors a few years ago. They were called Mitch's Sons-of-Bitches, which is pretty funny.

1943

March 11: Today is Mom's thirty-fifth birthday. Grant and I made a cake! (I must stop using exclamation points so much.) It was crooked but it tasted okay. Mom has a job at a food-packing plant, so I get supper started every day. I got a raise at the library, to 20 cents. Just about everything is rationed now: tea, coffee, sugar, and soon meat. Sometimes we can't get any sugar or potatoes or coal, even if we have the money. You can't get tires or gasoline, either, but we don't have a car so who cares? Dad says some people are making tons of money selling guns and munitions, while ordinary people just scrape along. Spinach is 19 cents, lettuce is a quarter. Mom says we can't afford it.

June 23: I stood first every month all year! I beat all the mean rich kids! . . . Billy Binks was killed. The second guy on our block. Bobby's mad and sad at the same time. His mouth goes shaky and his eyes scrunch up and he says he wants to kill Nazis.

August 29: Grant and I worked all summer at the United Church vacation school, looking after the little kids for $7.00 a month. With my library job (three days a week now) I should have enough to buy books for high school. I'm going to Jarvis Collegiate, not Central Tech like Grant. It's just a mile away so I can walk . . . Mom has a new job selling lingerie at Evangeline Shop, next to my all-time favourite place, Britnell's Book Store. She makes 40 cents an hour, which is pretty good. On Fridays she goes over to Jesse Ketchum School and serves lunch to kids whose mothers are in war plants. (I wonder about the other kids whose mothers work. Don't they count?) She also looks after the pamphlets and books and papers for the local branch of our new party, the Labour Progressive Party. They had a meeting at the King Eddy last week to get it going. (Uncle Bill came from Blairmore; he says they named a street after Tim Buck out there!) The Communist International is gone; now each country will have its own party, to work for socialism . . . The Nazis were pushed out of Africa; the *Star* says "the tide has turned."

October 30: High school is exciting and scary. On Day One we all had to take an IQ test, and the kids with the highest scores, including me, got put in Form 1E. We call ourselves the Brain Gang. They told us we're supposed to add to Jarvis's "glorious academic reputation," and win a bunch of scholarships. We said okay. Some kids from Rosedale are in my form: Fran, Cynthia (her father's a bigshot officer overseas), Marg, Bob W., Kitty. Paul C. and most of the English kids have gone back since the bombing isn't as bad . . . I've made a wonderful friend. Her name is Nicky, and she's smart and funny and daring, loves words and books, and believes in socialism. Her whole family is smaller than I am, and her mother calls me "koyn" (not sure of spelling — they use a different alphabet), which is Macedonian for "horse." I think we'll be friends for a long time . . . The Russians have driven the Germans almost to the Polish border. I wonder if Benny's grandparents are still alive. There are terrible rumours about German death camps . . . Had to answer the door. Susie for a bath. None too soon. She drops in once a month or so. Joe keeps asking her — in vain — to marry him. He's in the army, she's not sure where . . .

The Class of '43, Rosedale P.S.: I am standing, front row, centre, wearing a tunic. Seated in front are war refugees Michael (third from right) and Paul (second from right). Behind me is Cynthia, whose father was killed the same day the war ended.

1944

January 11: Hurray for the Revolution! Norman Freed and Charlie Sims got elected to city council! Mom and I worked hard canvassing and passing out leaflets — in wealthy Moore Park, of all places. Dad laughed and said, "Give not that which is holy unto the dogs." (That's from the Bible. I looked it up.) Nicky and I did the streets near Christie Pits. We gave each other courage . . . I did NOT stand first, I stood sixth, but when the whole class is brainy it's tough. I was first in French, though, with 96% . . . We have a combination radio-phonograph! It's super! For Christmas I got three Sinatra records ("Night and Day" makes my insides melt!), Artie Shaw's "Begin the Beguine," Count

Basie's "One O'Clock Jump," and Glenn Miller's "Moonlight Serenade." Dad taught me to dance and we have a party here almost every week. I kind of like Graham up the street, even though he wants to be an embalmer . . .

March 30: We've had snow for weeks. The streets are a mess and my feet get wet walking to school. I like every subject except Phys. Ed. which is pure torture. We're supposed to be able to stand up from a cross-legged sitting position. Nicky and I can't do it and we end up giggling and falling down. Miss S. has never giggled in her life . . . About standing up: there's a German kid in our class, Geraldine, who won't stand up for the anthem, and we're pretty mean to her. She's either stupid or brave, in a weird way. Mr. Nelson, our history teacher, is a madman. He was shell-shocked in the Great War, and every now and then he leaps up on his desk and starts shooting an imaginary machine gun at us. We topple into the aisles obediently. Then he yells, "Take cover, men!" and dives for the map closet. Yesterday Doug — who often amuses himself by mooing like a cow — locked him in. Mr. N. didn't seem to mind . . .

June 15: D-Day arrived! The second front, which the Party has been pushing for, opened June 6 with a massive invasion on the coast of France. It will make the Russians' job much easier. Everybody says Hitler is doomed. Nobody knows how many soldiers were killed — but we knew two of them. Bill and Fred Simpson, who helped us make those airplane models four years ago, died on the beach within minutes of each other. Grant and I cried a bit . . . That makes four boys killed on our own short block. Stupid, stupid war! . . . I was recommended. No exams to write.

September 17: I'm in Form 2C. Mr. Moorhouse is our homeroom teacher. We take Latin with him and I adore it. It's so elegant! We started German this year, too. Mr. Jenkins, the vice-principal, came in on the second day and said he'd understand if some of us objected to studying an enemy language, but then he said, "German is also the language of Goethe and Schiller and Wagner." Then he walked out. Most of us signed up right away. Miss St. John is our German teacher and she's a riot! She taught us to decline definite articles to the tune of "God Save the King": "der des dem den, die der/der die, das des dem den/die der den die." (Geraldine didn't stand up.) Crazy way to learn, but we don't forget. The other day she said, "Never touch a feminine in the singular!" The girls snickered, the boys hooted, and Doug mooed.

October 3: A strange thing: when Mr. Simpson heard about Bill and Fred, he died of a heart attack, and when his wife and his mother went to buy black dresses for his funeral, his mother collapsed and died. If you put that in a story, nobody would believe it . . .

December 21: I am now fourteen, *Gott sei dank!* Have also, in Mom's delicate phrase, "entered womanhood" (at last!). I was miserably self-conscious, felt as if everybody knew. I stood fourth this time, first in Latin and French, tied for first in German . . . Big assembly on Armistice Day. Mr. Jenkins read out the names of Jarvis grads and teachers killed so far. It was long . . .

1945

February 2: Yesterday went to the show (Embassy) with The Skunk. I made him beg for two days. *Thirty Seconds Over Tokyo,* with Van Johnson (Nicky is mad about him). The newsreel was better than the movie — first pictures of the Russian winter offensive, the biggest assault in history. Hundreds of thousands of soldiers, all in white, with their guns painted white, many on white skis — and they attacked in a blizzard along a 600-mile front. Joy came up in my throat . . .

April 25: Today is Dad's thirty-seventh birthday, and for a present he got fired. His company made tools that made cannons, and the war is almost over so they're laying people off. Isn't capitalism splendid? Mom's worried, has lost weight (I wish I could), says she doesn't know what we'll do. She makes $18.00 a week, and Grant and I make a few dollars and do the shopping and meals and dishes, but things will be tough. Dad's already pawned his watch, briefcase, and good fountain pen . . . A horrible thing happened: Joe was shipped home, called Susie from Halifax, and asked her for the hundredth time to marry him. She said no for the hundredth time — and then she heard a shot. He killed himself right there in the telephone booth. God!

May 8: It's over. The war in Europe is over. In the middle of our double Latin period this morning, the Hallelujah Chorus boomed out all through Jarvis. There was a hush for a second or two, and then we all cheered. Some kids, like Cynthia and Joan Rattray (war guest), cried. Even Mr. Moorhouse had *lacrimae* in his *oculi.* Everybody hugged everybody else — including Geraldine — and we were dismissed. Nicky and I went over to Yonge Street and walked downtown. It was jammed! Probably 50,000 people, half of them in uniform. We got kissed (and we kissed back — good practice!) as much as we could. People climbed lampposts and hung out of windows and danced till they dropped. Mosquito bombers flew low over the city and dropped miles of tickertape on us. It was wild! And so hard to believe . . .

May 10: Cynthia wasn't at school yesterday or today. They just found out that her father was killed the same day the war ended . . .

May 17: Nicky and I took a long lunch hour today. Somebody said bubblegum was back in the stores, so we went looking. Didn't get back till two o'clock. We were sent to Jenkins's office, scared out of our minds. He asked where we'd been, and we told him, and he put his hand over his mouth. I think he was laughing. But then he looked at us sternly and said, "What am I going to do with you? There's no point in giving you a detention or extra work. You don't need it." Then he looked at us again, for a long, long minute, and sighed, and said, "Go back to class." Whew!

July 12: I passed with honours, 89% average, no exams, and now I have a job at Honey Dew, the big one at Carlton and Yonge. Pay is 30 cents an hour, and I work about twenty hours a week, clearing dishes, and taking orders to tables. On my third day a little man in a grey suit came in, placed an order at the counter, and sat down. The manager got all excited and said it was E. P. Taylor, who owns Honey Dew and half of Canada. I took his order to him: one poached egg, unbuttered brown toast, tea. It's the first time I've seen a capitalist up close. I wasn't impressed. I was even less impressed when he didn't leave a tip . . . Russia counted up its dead: 20,000,000 . . .

August 15: It's finished. Japan surrendered yesterday. On August 6, the United States dropped a strange and powerful bomb made from uranium on Hiroshima, and three days later another on Nagasaki. Both cities have vanished. Nobody knows how many men and women and children were incinerated. The *Star* said 150,000, with 100,000 badly burnt or injured. The newsreels and photos summon up horror and awe. Why? Why, with Russia ready to invade? Why, with Japan on its knees? Why?

CLAIRE MACKAY *graduated from the University of Toronto in 1952, with an honours degree in political science and economics. Her extensive résumé includes six years as research librarian for the Steelworkers' Union. In her writing career, Claire became a historian, novelist and short-story writer, winner of the Ruth Schwartz Award, the City of Toronto Award of Merit, and both Vicky Metcalf awards (for body of work and for short story). Claire is a mini-bike aficionada (that means a female lover of mini-bikes) who is* Bats About Baseball. *She is the mother of mystery writer Scott, and daughter of nonagenarian (that means a person between ninety and one hundred years old) Bernice Bacchus, whose war-time journals and remarkable memory helped in the research for this chapter. Claire is a founding member and past president of CANSCAIP (the Canadian Society of Children's Authors, Illustrators and Performers). She still does not care for capitalists.*

BUDGE WILSON

To live in Halifax, Nova Scotia, is to be aware of the shadow of war — even in peacetime.

Point Pleasant Park, on the tip end of the city, with water on three sides, is full of giant trees and meandering paths. It is also sprinkled with old forts. Cannons sit side by side with park benches and picnic tables. As a kid, I loved climbing over the huge guns and jumping down from the high places on the forts. Sometimes we could even go inside, where everything was dark, damp, and full of untold stories. It was my dad who took me to those places.

As long ago as I can remember, you could see battleships lined up near the Narrows, just before the harbour widens out into Bedford Basin. During my lifetime, there have always been bases for soldiers, airmen, and, of course, the navy. And towering above the town, visible for miles, rises massive Citadel Hill, with its Dry Ditch moat, drawbridge, huge guns, and all the other paraphernalia of war. I used to play on the Citadel with my best friend, Molly, walking along the edges of the deep moat, looking at Hangman's Beach out near the horizon, sitting on the rickety stone stairways. From the Citadel, we could see everything: the "city of trees," the huge Basin, the wide open sea.

Besides these more obvious scenes of war were other tales — about the Halifax Explosion. On a cold December day in 1917, one-third of the city was levelled when the collision of a Belgian Relief ship and a munitions vessel caused a massive explosion. It was the largest man-made explosion before the first nuclear bomb was detonated. Over two thousand people were killed and nine thousand wounded. Six thousand homes were destroyed. Hundreds of people were blinded by flying glass when they rushed to the windows to watch the burning ships.

Moments before the explosion, my own mother left her typewriter to get something in another office, thereby escaping the huge window that blew in over her desk. She was young then, not yet married. Years later, I remember meeting a little girl my own age at a music festival. We both felt jittery about playing on a real grand piano in front of all those people. I was horrified to learn that her mother — blinded in the Explosion — had never seen her. There she was in her patent leather shoes, all decked out in a party dress, getting ready to play her piece. Who picked out the dress? Who admired it? Who was there to tell her she looked pretty? Sixty years later, I'm still haunted by that little girl and her mother.

Tales about the Halifax Explosion were part of the folklore of my childhood, with vivid accounts of the victims — screaming, bleeding, staggering — struggling through the wreckage and the fires to the hospitals. It was our mothers who told us those stories of death and destruction. Few of our fathers had experienced it. They had been off in Europe at that time, fighting in World War I — ironically referred to as "the war to end all wars."

My father, an almost unfailingly cheerful person, refused to tell me stories about that war. I begged him to do so, but he would not. I wanted to hear tales of heroism and danger, but he, knowing that war was neither thrilling nor romantic, kept silent. I knew he'd won a medal. What was it for? What had he done to deserve it? He had received a severe wound to his knee.

What had caused it? He ignored my questions.

On September 10, 1939, I passed the open door of our den, the room where we listened to the radio, sat by the fire, talked. My cheerful father was sitting in his special chair, bent over, his head in his hands. He may have been crying. The radio was on, announcing that war had just been declared. I was only twelve, but I recognized the reasons for his pain. He knew things about war that I did not, and those things were too awful to speak about. Now, all that terrible experience was about to be repeated. I didn't go in and speak to him. I knew he needed to be alone.

Halifax was no longer training for war, playing at war, remembering war. It was *at* war. In 1939, the route across the Atlantic was not by air. It was by sea. Montreal, with the closest well-equipped port facilities, had a harbour that froze over in the wintertime. Halifax Harbour stayed open. Halifax thus became the gateway to the battle areas of England and Europe. A flyer entitled *Air Raid Precautions — Instructions* was circulated throughout the city. The document started with the following words: "The Province of Nova Scotia has been designated as an area liable to enemy attack. Protect yourself and your community . . ."

Can you imagine what it felt like to read that when you were only twelve years old? Visualize, if you can, a city of sixty thousand people, crowded almost entirely onto a small peninsula, surrounded on three sides by the sea, joined to the rest of the province by a relatively narrow neck. On a map, Halifax looks like a giant mushroom. At that time, that neck or stem of land contained the only two roads leading out of the city. I was to think of that fact often in the next six years. What if there were another explosion, or maybe a fire that could destroy that whole city of wooden houses? What of the risk of invasion from across the sea? How could so many people escape along those two roads? And where would they go? Molly and I discussed all those alarming things.

Imagine now what happens when a city of that size and shape doubles its population. Because that's what happened. It seemed as though everywhere we looked we saw some sort of serviceman, or, less frequently, service woman. We kids had a game that we often played. You closed your eyes, turned around several times, and then opened your eyes. If you didn't see someone in uniform, you lost a point. But regardless of where you were in the city, you almost always did see one — or a dozen of them.

Sailors from France in their red pom-pom hats walked our downtown streets beside soldiers and airmen from a score of other countries. Our own sailors in their tight middy tops and bell bottom trousers were everywhere. I liked them best, with their swagger and their rolling gait. In Bedford Basin, as many as one hundred ships would be gathering and waiting — often more. The trains brought carloads of men from all across Canada. At a secret but appointed time, they would leave Halifax in those ships, sliding out of Bedford Basin into the main harbour, and then out to sea, in their silent ominous convoys. From the Citadel, or down by the Park, we watched them go.

A convoy gathers inBedford Basin.

We knew we were witnessing high drama, and the fact that the drama was coupled with potential tragedy probably made the sight more thrilling to us. Supply ships and war vessels — large and small — were painted with weird camouflaging lines and zigzag stripes in order to be less visible on a wavy sea. Their departure was top secret, and we didn't speak of it. But we had eyes. We could see.

A Cross-roads of the World: An influx of military personnel doubled the population of Halifax during the war years. Drawing by Robert Chambers, 1943.

As a young girl of twelve, I romanticized a lot about what I was watching. Much of what was happening was exciting to me and to my friends. The full horror and ugliness of war took awhile to become real to us. I knew of these things with the surface of my mind, but my twelve-year-old heart was not breaking. I loved the swarms of handsome men in their various uniforms, strolling up and down the streets of my town. I longed to be one of those "Wrens" in their snappy little hats, going off to mysterious adventures across the seas. I wanted to be a spy; I knew I was ready to cope with deprivation and cold and pain. I'd survive. I felt invincible.

The young boys and men felt the same way. They ached to be flipping through the skies in those agile little fighter planes, or marching to victory with guns in their hands — preferably with bagpipes blowing in front of them. We were used to colourful and musical military parades in Halifax. For a while, we failed to notice that the soldiers did not march off to war with bands playing. Everything was done in such secrecy that few of us saw them arriving or leaving. They were spirited out to their ships without the comfort or inspiration of music. But for a short while, our young minds seemed oblivious to either death or mutilation or fear.

I couldn't see why our parents wouldn't let Molly and me walk alone in Point Pleasant Park — 186 acres of wooded land surrounded by sea. I felt profound outrage at that unnecessary restriction, that humiliating caution. I was strong and agile. If anyone grabbed me, I knew I could escape. I could slap, scratch, kick. I'd be fine. Then, one day, I was chased by a soldier on a sunny afternoon on a secluded residential street. What could have been safer than that time and that place? He almost caught me, and I can still remember my terror before he gave up the chase. I didn't argue with my mother anymore about Point Pleasant Park.

We knew that life was far from fun for the armed service personnel in Halifax. We knew this because in our overcrowded city, our own citizens now experienced similar discomforts. There weren't enough restaurants; there were no public bars or taverns, and too few movie theatres to accommodate so many people. The transportation system — the "Banana Special" fleet of rattling yellow streetcars — was stretched beyond its limits, with neither resources nor manpower for expansion. You either walked or you waited. It was a city bursting at the seams.

But much that was happening was undeniably exciting. Tons of bolts of thick black fabric were made available for blackout curtains, and we were required to cover every window at night, so that our lights would be invisible from sky or sea. Outside, it was inky black. To save power, daylight saving and standard times were increased by an extra hour. I walked the mile to school in the dark on many winter mornings. I loved that. It added one more adventure to my day.

At night, in the midst of the darkness, the searchlights practised their manoeuvres in the murky sky. Like a set of giant Northern Lights, the beams crossed and criss-crossed each other above us, searching for the planes that were always up there. We could hear them. When they caught a plane in their weaving search, the craft was dramatically illuminated — a sitting duck. We weren't so young and callous that we didn't realize that this was how planes could be discovered and shot down. The searchlights were hunting. The planes were hiding. They were preparing for the real thing. I spent a lot of time at night outside, watching the spectacle. If my parents wondered what I was doing out there — all alone, staring at the sky — they didn't ask. On nights when the air raid sirens were practising, filling the city with their agonized wail, the real thing seemed very close. In fact, the real thing *was* extremely close. As the weeks and months passed, people with a good view of the sea beyond the harbour's mouth could see fires, explosions, signs that the Nazi submarines had found their targets.

In the meantime, our mothers were knitting up a storm — making mittens, balaclava caps, and scarves, mostly for the navy men doomed to the bitter winter cold of the North Atlantic. These women worked long hours each week at the hostels and canteens for the people in the armed forces, handing out coffee, mending rips and tears, making sandwiches, hoping they'd get home in time to look after their own families. My mother, frail and nervous at the best of times, seemed to be tired more often than not. On weekends, men and women from the navy, air force, and army came into our homes for meals, to sink into comfortable armchairs to tell their tales, to have a bath. One sailor, a frequent visitor when his boat was in port, would walk into our house and run upstairs to turn on the bath water before he even stopped to say hello.

We loved those armed service people who came to share our family with us. My sister was five years older than I, so while I had heroes, she had dates. Off she went with those very young men — to stand in line for a movie, to go dancing, to talk to them over coffee. I was too young for any of that wonderful stuff, but I could watch and listen when they came to visit us. These were people with stories to tell. Later on, when I was older, I was often reminded of those lines from *Othello*: "She loved me for the dangers I had pass'd." For a time, it just seemed to be danger we heard about. It took awhile for death to become familiar to us.

Then the English Guest Children began to arrive, sent to Canada to be safe from the bombs in their own country. Hundreds of them came, and they were fanned out over the whole land, where host families took them in for the war's duration. My own school seemed to be full of them. They became a crucial element in my journey through and out of childhood. They arrived — homesick and alien — to a country that had no idea who or what it was receiving.

Because their British educational system was superior to ours, the new arrivals were often shoved ahead into classes of students who were two years older than they were. Never mind that they were socially naive by our standards and were often not even comfortable with their own peers in Canada. The British class system stayed firmly in place, even in a foreign land. Feelings of superiority or inferiority surfaced as the English children assessed each others' accents. Were they high or low class? Were they country or city bred? Those kids could tell, and for them it mattered.

English Guest Children — homesick and alien — landed in Halifax and were fanned out across the country.

Among Canadians, the guests were painfully conscious that their clothes were strange, their way of speaking noticeable, their customs different from ours — in food, in dress, in behaviour. And the homes in which they found themselves were not always kind.

If one were looking for heroism, one could find it in those kids — and in their parents who sent them to us, knowing that the children they would receive back would be vastly changed. Long years later, when I became a parent myself, I thought often about the selfless sacrifice of those mothers and fathers. Some of the children who returned home at the end of the war eventually repacked their suitcases and came back to Canada to live out the rest of their lives in this country. I still ache for their parents.

Many Canadian kids had a love-hate relationship with the Guest Children. In spite of the fact that they tended to look and act much younger than we did (with their short pants, their prim pigtails, their little belted coats, and their bowler hats), they often had an air of conscious superiority about them which was both maddening and captivating. They could run rings around us in French, in mathematics, in English literature. They could beat us in every sport we played. We couldn't sort out the various accents we heard, so most of them sounded like dukes and duchesses to us. They were feisty and equipped with stiff upper lips. They neither complained nor wept — not in our presence anyway. They were a formidable lot.

I think we often found them too admirable. They made us feel like spoiled brats. We certainly must have looked like that to them, and maybe that's exactly what we were. We envied them their scary first-hand experiences of the war and the adventures they were able to describe. We didn't like it that they were smarter and more athletic than we were. But I didn't tell my parents — or even Molly — about my negative feelings. Kids often wear special masks in front of their families and friends.

But we also loved the guests and respected them. We copied a number of their British expressions and bought clothes that were simpler, more basic than ours. I remember looking in vain in our stores for one of those little belted coats. We listened to their stories of air raids and the whistling bombs, and felt grudging admiration.

They did the same sort of crossover thinking as we did. They saw that it was normal for boys and girls to be attracted to one another at thirteen and fourteen. The girls cut and permed their hair; the boys got long pants. They were envious of our freer, less formal ways of dress and behaviour; they grew to admire a country in which one's worth wasn't assessed by the way one spoke. They went camping and canoeing and came to love the wilderness; they learned how to skate; they finally succeeded in liking peanut butter. They never got over being thrilled by snow. For all of us, it was a time of conflict, affection, and intense personal growth.

Of course, we all learned about ration stamps, limits on a lot of products needed in the war, shortages of certain luxury items, war savings certificates. But these things seemed increasingly unimportant, as news started to arrive about boys and men whom we knew being killed, maimed, blinded. Increasingly, enemy activity outside the giant surface-to-sea-bottom gate across the mouth of Halifax Harbour was close enough to be witnessed at night.

One Sunday evening, after his parents had been hosting servicemen, my husband — at age fourteen — said goodbye to a sailor friend who was going down to the docks to rejoin his ship — a minesweeper. Two hours later, from his bedroom on a hill in Dartmouth, he saw the vessel's departure from the harbour. Then he watched in horror as his friend's ship exploded before his very eyes. That's how close submarine activity was to the cities of Halifax and Dartmouth.

From time to time, danger seemed even closer. We were used to the constant testing of air raid sirens, but we weren't used to gunfire. I know exactly where I was on the night I heard the sound of heavy guns down by the harbour. It went on and on, and it wasn't hard to think, "They've come. They're invading Halifax." Hearing it, the English Guest Children must have wondered why they had bothered to leave home. In the morning, we learned that a munitions ship, the *Trongate,* had caught fire in the harbour. The guns we had heard were real ones — our own. Fearing another massive Halifax Explosion, our own armed forces were sinking the ship by pumping it full of what seemed like limitless rounds of ammunition. Those who were close enough to see the activity watched, transfixed, as giant flames shot into the sky and sounds of small explosions filled the air. Had they not been successful in sinking the vessel, the result could have been an explosion even more destructive than the first one in 1917. As well as being in a position to endanger the city's core, the ship was surrounded by two hundred other boats in the harbour that night.

At the age of sixteen, I spent two months in the coastal village of Hubbards, where a school had been set up to train young men for service in Canada's Merchant Navy — to man the supply ships that were so crucial to the war effort. The students were eighteen or nineteen years old and came from all parts of Canada. During the day, they worked in the classrooms or on the training vessels. In the evenings, they danced in the Iona dance hall with the local girls or drank Coke with them at Scottie's busy coffee bar. Warm friendships were formed at that time, and for several years I corresponded with one of the students. He eventually commanded his own ship, sending me letters and gifts from exotic places around the world. Now — fifty-five years later — I often wonder if he is one of those who are lobbying the government for recognition and some compensation for their dangerous work and sacrifices during the war.

When I was seventeen, I went to school in Ontario. My father spent a period of time as Chairman of the War Labour Board, and we had to live in Ottawa for a while. Therefore I was absent from Halifax on VE Day — the day the Germans surrendered, thereby ending the European part of the war. But I learned about what happened that day — from newspapers, from the radio, from letters.

After a few hours of harmless celebration in the city, suddenly the mood changed. Remembering the difficult overcrowded years in Halifax, with long line-ups at restaurants and theatres, and no places to enjoy a quiet beer, large groups of sailors broke into the liquor stores and started passing out the bottles. Then the rioting began. With more and more people getting drunk, they started to take out six years of frustration on the merchants of downtown

Halifax, smashing storefronts and making off with jewellery, furs, and all manner of merchandise. It was a terrifying and ugly scene. Members of the armed forces started the destruction, but many citizens of the city — triggered by a crazy mob psychology — joined in the vandalism and the looting. The hysteria soon spread to Dartmouth, where similar events took place.

Young people looked on in shock and disillusionment as military personnel, school teachers, respected citizens were seen leaving stores with their arms full of stolen goods. Many of these items were returned to the stores in the following days, by people who were ashamed to discover what they were capable of. But some of those who witnessed the VE Day Riots learned things that day which changed forever their view of the trust they could place in family, mentors, and friends.

When I returned to Halifax in late June, most of the storefronts were still boarded up, and the downtown area looked like a ghost town.

That summer, I went back to Ontario to work at one of Ontario's Farmerette Camps, set up to harvest the crops on the rich farmland beside Lake Ontario, close to St. Catharines. All of us were high-school students, sixty of whom went out every day to work on neighbouring farms. Five of us were called Camp Assistants — a fancy title. What we did was keep the place clean and prepare the food for the other sixty kids. Scrubbing barracks floors and cleaning the outdoor toilets, we became intimately familiar with Dustbane and bulk soaps, as well as DDT, which was sprayed liberally around the kitchen area. We got athlete's foot in the showers. We peeled sixty-six potatoes a night. One of us got blood poisoning from a cut.

The work team takes a break. I am second from the left.

We knew what was meant by "a mountain of dishes."

At that camp I discovered what hard work could really be like, putting in a twelve-hour day, then sometimes going out to work in the orchards when the trees were loaded down with overripe fruit. Or we hitchhiked to Port Dalhousie's Lakeland Amusement Park or to a movie in St. Catharines. I shudder now to think of the danger we were in, accepting drives from whoever was willing to pick us up, not knowing if the driver was drunk or sober until we got in the car. Once we drove home in the back of a manure truck. Other drives were scarier. We'd arrive back at the camp at midnight or later; then the alarm would ring at 5 a.m., and another day would begin. At seven o'clock each morning, a radio program started with an aggravating theme that we all grew to hate, urging us to get up and start the day with a song.

We'd already been up for two hours. We felt like throwing our scrub buckets at the radio. Today, over fifty years later, I can still hear that tune in my head.

One morning, while I was at the camp, the radio reported that the "Magazine" — the munitions storage area close to Halifax and Dartmouth — was on fire, and that an enormous explosion was feared. The citizens of Halifax and Dartmouth, the news reporter told us, were already being evacuated from the two cities. A mushroom cloud hung over Dartmouth and Halifax. I thought about the first Explosion that had killed and wounded so many people. I remembered that narrow neck of land joining Halifax to the mainland, and visualized thousands of people streaming out those two roads. I was terrified for my city.

Then one of the girls said, "Oh, well. I've heard that Halifax people treated the armed forces really badly during the war." I was speechless. So much for the efforts of our mothers and fathers to help in any way they could during those six long years. Let the city explode. Let dead bodies line the streets. They deserve it. I could think of nothing to say.

The explosions, although immensely loud and colourful (according to my husband, who helped in the evacuation of the citizens of Dartmouth), did not escalate into a major catastrophe. Nonetheless, when I returned to Halifax in late August, the storefront windows of the downtown district were boarded up once more. The explosions did at least that much damage. The houses that were evacuated that night were left open in order to lessen the effects of a possible major explosion. (Closed windows will smash more easily than open ones.) The sailors, who had been the chief instigators of the VE Day Riots, were exceptionally helpful and orderly during the crisis, volunteering their efforts to protect people's homes, keeping watch throughout the night. My husband's father reported one of them as having said to him, "Figured we owed you one." Many fences were mended during that long and frightening evening.

July 18, 1945: a mushroom cloud hung over Dartmouth and Halifax. The explosions, although immensely loud and colourful, did not escalate into a major catastrophe.

By the time VJ Day arrived and the war in the Pacific ended, the mood was quieter — more one of relief and thankfulness than wild, excessive celebration. And the bombing of Hiroshima and Nagasaki filled me with deep doubts and a guilt that I still feel. Nevertheless, I celebrated with some young friends on the beach at Hubbards, grouped around a big bonfire, beside the sounds of the sea. I had just turned eighteen. One of my friends had lost her two brothers in the war. She didn't attend that party.

There was an aftermath to the war that was a wonderful bonus for some of us who had been too young to fight. Those of us who went on to university that fall found ourselves in the company of hundreds of mature men and women — the veterans, or vets — who were continuing their education after experiencing years of fear and courage and bitter adventure. These were not naive and gangly youths, but seasoned adults, old before their time. The university girls took pleasure in the fact that at Dalhousie University there were 7.4 men per female student! In classes, the vets were unusually confident and forthcoming in their views. In the coffee shop, intense discussions took place — about life, death, and the ultimate meaning of our humanity. I enjoyed this amazing atmosphere for four years. The vets seldom talked about the war. But the experience had matured them, sometimes in a destructive way, but more often in a sober, thoughtful way. It was a privilege to attend university during those years.

So, am I glad that I lived in Halifax during and after World War II? Yes, I am. No sane person would ever want a war to happen — especially that one, with its appalling damage to people and places and the human spirit. But if something of that magnitude happens, I want to have been close enough to experience at least a part of it. I'm sorry I missed witnessing the VE Day Riots, awful though they were. I wish I had felt the terror and seen and heard the fires and explosions of the ammunition storage area, filling the air with spectacular sound and light. To a writer, almost everything can be the raw material of fiction. I used my experiences of wartime Halifax in writing my children's novel *Thirteen Never Changes.* When I finished it, I could feel that in some mysterious way, one of my wheels had come full circle.

Being there can provide other strange satisfactions. If, on VE Day, I had witnessed that grim example of what some social scientists would call "Group Contagion," I might now have a better understanding of what exactly happens when a crowd goes crazy. I might be able to disentangle some of the causes of raw violence, and come closer to comprehending the roots of random acts of vandalism and hate.

And if I had experienced the terror of that July night, when many people feared that Halifax and Dartmouth were on the brink of a second major explosion, I might have found it easier — then and now — to analyze and cope with my own small anxieties. If I had seen the sky light up with the fires and heard the thunder of the explosions, I might have learned that even at the most terrible of moments, there can be a kind of awful beauty.

It is true that Halifax was not in the centre of a major war zone. But it was close, very close. It was on the edge, just as we were on the edge of childhood and very close to adulthood by the time the war ended. I'm glad that I was there.

BUDGE WILSON *took psychology, philosophy, and education at Dalhousie University after the war. She then lived in Ontario for over thirty years, working as commercial artist, teacher, secretary, and photographer; she was a fitness instructor for over twenty years. Her first novel was published in 1984, and she has since produced twenty-one books. Her awards include the CBC Short Fiction Award, City of Dartmouth Book Award, Canadian Library Association Young Adult Book Award, and the Ann Connor Brimer Award.*

She and her husband, Alan Wilson, returned home in 1989, and live in a fishing village on Nova Scotia's South Shore. They have two daughters and two grandsons. Budge consulted Alan's memoir in Children's Voices in Atlantic Literature and Culture *for some details of the VE Day riots and the 1945 Explosion. She writes in a tiny cabin that Alan built for her, overlooking Northwest Cove and St. Margaret's Bay.*

BRIAN DOYLE

It's hot today.

On the way to getting ice for the ice box I'm telling Chicken Tetrazini about the two Alan Ladd movies I saw yesterday at the Rat Hole. Actually, it's called the Rialto but everybody calls it the Rat Hole because it's so dirty and sometimes you feel the rats jumping around your feet fighting over the popcorn on the floor. Chicken couldn't see the movies because we didn't have enough money for the both of us. We only had enough for one of us to go. That's what we sometimes do. One of us gets to go to the show and then tells the other one about what happened. It's usually me that gets to go because I'm better at telling. Chicken isn't very good at telling because he gets too excited. Chicken's real name is Anthony. Anthony Tetrazini.

When Chicken starts to tell he starts worrying about telling. Then he jumps all around in the story, telling the end first, then the start, then leaving out important parts, and then maybe he forgets what happened altogether. By that time nobody wants to listen anymore to Chicken and your mind starts to go other places and you start thinking about Claudette who lives up over the store and doesn't wear any underpants.

The best way to tell is to start right in the middle, then tell a little bit, then go right back to the very start and go ahead to the middle again and then shoot right through to the end. That's the way I do it.

I hate going to get the ice. The ice house is away over on St. Anthony Street, about ten blocks from where I live at 32 Cobourg Street near St. Patrick. By the time you get the ice home it's almost all melted.

Chicken pulls the wagon and I tell. I need both hands to tell. I use my hands when I talk. It's two Alan Ladd movies I have to tell. It was supposed to be three but one of them burned up. There was smoke coming out of the projection room at the back of the Rat Hole.

When I got in my seat it was the middle of *This Gun for Hire,* and I was happy because that's where I like to start. When it was over they put on *The Glass Key,* and when *The Glass Key* was over they put on *This Gun for Hire* again instead of the other Alan Ladd movie that was supposed to be on — *Salty O'Rourke* it was called. The Rat Hole was full of smoke. As soon as *This Gun for Hire* came on everybody started yelling and hollering and throwing stuff so the movie got shut off and somebody turned on all the lights and the manager got up on the stage and told us that there'd only be *two* Alan Ladd movies today because the other one caught fire and burned up and he wasn't going to give anybody their money back and if we didn't like it we could all just go home and forget about it and then the lights went out and they started up *This Gun for Hire* again from the beginning and I stayed right to the end so I saw the second half twice. This way I'd remember it better when I was telling it all to Chicken Tetrazini.

Today, Chicken is mad because we didn't get our money back. He put in seven cents and I put in eight. There was one cent left over. I bought a grab bag with it and shared the candy with Chicken outside before I went into the show. He took the blackballs and I had the rest. That was OK. I don't like blackballs. They turn your mouth and your teeth all black.

Veronica Lake is always in the movies with Alan Ladd. Her long hair always falls over her right eye and her lips are very curly in the middle. Chicken likes to hear about that. About her long hair over her eye and her curly lips. We're down near the corner of Cobourg and St. Patrick going by Mrs. Tubbs's house. She's got flags hanging out all her windows and streamers on her porch. And she's got a picture of her son, Wash, in the window. His real name isn't Wash, it's Flight Lieutenant Terence Tubbs. Everybody on Cobourg Street calls him Wash. Even his mother and father. Wash joined the Air Force last year. He's only sixteen. Well, he's seventeen now. He got to be a pilot right away. Everybody says he's too young but it doesn't matter now because the war is over.

It said on the radio last night at seven o'clock that the war was over. A big announcement. We had to miss *The Lone Ranger* because of it. Everybody was cheering and running in and out of their houses and up and down the street.

Mrs. Tubbs is happy. She's waving out the window at us as we go by with my wagon. She's happy because the war's over and Wash Tubbs will soon be home. Her son.

Last week they dropped two atom bombs on Japan and killed everybody.

That's why all of a sudden the war's over. They couldn't take it anymore.

There's going to be a big party on Cobourg Street tonight. Everybody's talking about it.

Maybe even Wash Tubbs will be home from the war in time for the party tonight.

I'm telling Chicken Tetrazini about the Alan Ladd movie *The Glass Key.* Alan Ladd wore a long coat with big shoulders for the whole movie even when he was inside people's houses. And he only had his hat off once in the whole movie, when he was half dead in the hospital. No, another time he had his hat *and* coat off was when William Bendix — playing handball with Alan Ladd — was throwing him up against the wall like a rubber ball, and, oh yes, another time when two other guys threw him in a tub of cold water. It's hard to keep your hat on when you are getting thrown into a tub of water. William Bendix put a whole onion in a sandwich and stuffed it in his mouth all at once, he's such a pig, and meanwhile Alan Ladd set fire to the mattress he was tied to and crashed out the window and through a glass skylight and escaped. His face was a mess, but the next day in the hospital when Veronica Lake came in to visit him he looked like his old handsome self again. She almost kissed him right there in the hospital bed. You could tell by the music and the way her curly lips were about two stories high on the screen.

Everybody at the show liked it when Alan Ladd said "thanks!" with his beautiful deep voice. "Thanks!" He said "thanks!" in the movie about fifty times and whenever he said it everybody got very quiet.

Next, William Bendix wants to play handball with Alan Ladd again but William Bendix is too drunk and while I'm telling Chicken this, I'm thinking about a girl at York Street School, Shelley Mayburger, who had her very own picture of Alan Ladd. A big picture in a frame with glass on it her mother bought her for her eleventh birthday at Woolworth's on Rideau Street. Shelley brought it to school one day and put it on her desk and was kissing it while the teacher was telling us about the war and the teacher saw her and went quiet and then turned purple and took it away from her and fired it in the basket.

And I'm telling Chicken Tetrazini about how William Bendix choked his boss to death after he played handball with Alan Ladd and then the cops came and Alan Ladd went off to get married to Veronica Lake.

We're in the ice house yard on St. Andrew Street and I give the dime my mother gave me to the guy in the office and he gives me a ticket.

In the office there's two other guys drinking beer and talking about the war being over and how they wish they could've gone to it but they were too old. Then one of them comes out and we go into the ice house with my wagon and he brushes away the sawdust. It smells like wet wood and some kind of cold flowers and something dark like bark but it's not that and he cuts off a piece of broken ice that's only half the size it's supposed to be for a dime and with his ice tongs drops it in my wagon. I hate this guy. He's always giving me the smallest block he can find and by the time I get it home it's even smaller and everybody's mad at me.

This is why I hate going for ice.

"Can't you give me a bigger block?" I say.

He looks at me like I'm some kind of a bedbug or something.

Then he grabs the ice out of my wagon with the tongs and gives me another piece. This one's even smaller!

"Why ain't you two over fightin' the Japs?" he says to me and Chicken Tetrazini. "Maybe you should grow up a bit first, eh?" Then he laughs just like William Bendix did when he threw Alan Ladd through the big glass window.

On the way back home we try to pull the wagon under as many trees as we can to keep the sun off the ice but pretty soon the wagon is leaking water and leaving a trail and the ice is getting smaller in the heat and there's nothing we can do about it.

In *This Gun for Hire* Alan Ladd is a bad guy who gets up in the morning with all his clothes on and puts on his long coat and his gun and his hat and gives his little kitten some milk and pets it and shoots a guy for some reason and also the guy's secretary who is trying to make Alan Ladd a coffee.

Veronica Lake is a singer who does magic tricks while she's singing to old drunks at the tables. Alan Ladd gets on a train beside Veronica Lake who is a spy for the war.

"You talkin' to me?" Alan Ladd says to Veronica Lake. I say the same thing to Chicken just like Alan Ladd says it.

"You talkin' to me?" In my real deep voice.

Alan Ladd says "thanks!" a whole lot more times, and I tell Chicken again how everybody at the show got real quiet when he said it in his deep voice. I say to Chicken, "Do you like the way I'm telling the movies?"

"Yes, I do," says Chicken.

"Thanks!" I say, in my best real deep voice. My Alan Ladd voice.

On St. Patrick Street they're organizing a parade because the war's over. The street is full of torn paper and bottles and confetti and glass from last night when everybody ran out into the street and got drunk because the war is over.

Veronica Lake gets kidnapped by Alan Ladd and leaves a trail of her magician's cards for the cops to follow.

She could have had a wagon of melting ice — that would've left a pretty good trail!

Alan Ladd is hiding in a chemical factory which is full of barrels of poison gas that the enemy is going to use to kill everybody.

Veronica Lake gets a twisted ankle and her hair falls over her right eye and her mouth gets quite curly. A fat guy who eats peppermints all the time is a traitor and the cops come and gun down Alan Ladd who can't sleep because his cat died.

Veronica Lake says, "You saved my life," and Alan Ladd, even though he's dead, says "thanks!" and it's the end.

We stop and talk to some of Chicken's friends from the Catholic School, St. Brigid's, about the parade. They're going to have their own parade tonight and if we want we can go in it if we bring something to make noise with.

Near the corner of St. Patrick and Cobourg some people in front of the fish store are building a thing you hang people from on a hay wagon and painting a sign that says "HAN," so far.

By the time we get home all I've got is a wagon full of water. Well, not exactly. There's a piece of ice left about the size of a baseball in the wagon rolling around up to its waist in water.

Chicken says he has to go home because his mother has a job for him but I know it's because he doesn't want to be at my place when my father sees this block of ice.

I'm lucky. My father's gone to the Lafayette Beer Parlour.

My mother looks at the ice.

My mother's belly is so big she can hardly walk. The baby was supposed to come out last week, the day they dropped the first bomb on Japan and killed everybody. But the baby stayed in.

Scared maybe.

She says she knows the baby is a boy. How does she know? She just knows. She knows it will be a boy. A little brother for me.

She looks at the ice.

"Disgraceful," she says. She picks up the bit of ice with one hand and opens the top of the ice box and puts it carefully in there beside the butter. She shakes her head. "Maybe now that the war's over they'll have time to put those ice house pickpockets in jail!"

I decide to go up to the Union Station and watch the soldiers come in.

I often do that. There's always a big crowd there. And sometimes my father's third cousin once removed, Doug Holmes, will give me some money. He's a red cap there. Carries people's suitcases. His pocket is always jingling with money. And he stutters. When he gives me the handful of money out of his pocket he never looks at it. And he always says, "Say hello to your f . . . f . . . f . . ." He can't seem to say "father" so I always say, "my father, OK, I will say hello to my father." But I never do. What's the use of saying hello to your own father?

I walk over Anglesea Square and past my school and up York Street towards the Byward Market. On the corner of York and Friel Street there's Shelley Mayburger sitting on her front step. She gets up and walks along with me.

"How's Anthony?" she says. She means Chicken Tetrazini. She likes Chicken. She's always asking me about him. He can't stand her.

"Anthony who?" I say.

"Anthony Tetrazini," she says.

"Oh, you mean Chicken Tetrazini!" I say.

"Why do you call him Chicken?"

I don't answer her. A bunch of people are making a huge body out of straw and old clothes. There's a sign beside the straw body. "Hirohito" the sign says.

"What's Hirohito?" Shelley says.

"Hirohito is the Emperor of Japan," I say.

"What are they doing?" she says. "What's everybody doing? And last night. All the noise and singing. I thought I was having a nightmare!"

"The war is over," I say.

"The war is over?" she says. No wonder Chicken doesn't like her.

Shelley goes up Dalhousie Street towards Rideau to see what's all the racket up there, and I walk up York to the Lafayette Beer Parlour. There's a big fan vent flapping away in the wall beside the door blowing cigarette smoke and beer fumes and stomach gas out onto the street. There's a roar of talking and shouting behind the door. I push open the door and stick my head in to see if I can see my father. The beer fumes and farts and belches and smoke hit me in the face like a slab of wood. I can't see if he's in there or not. The place is full of men and smoke and shouting and laughing and bottles and glasses rattling and pounding. The men at the table near the door look at my head peeking in.

"Get out!" they all say. "Come back in ten years!" and then they all laugh. I shut the door.

"Hello, f . . . f . . . f . . . father," I say to myself and head over to the Union Station.

It's hot today.

My father always says it's so hot you could fry an egg on the sidewalk. And I always say I would try it but we haven't got any eggs. And my mother always says soon the war will be over and we'll have all the eggs we want. Well, now the war is over and I guess the eggs will be along pretty soon. And my father would probably say, "The chickens'll have to arrive on the scene first."

On the doors of Woolworth's on Rideau Street there are some printed signs on stuck paper.

FOR SALE. One Air Force Officer's Uniform (ask inside)

BED-BUG KILLER — $2.50 a gallon

Girl to Iron, Wash Dishes, Twice Weekly Evenings
30 cents per hr.

1937 DeSoto — $500.00

Bed Sitting Room — 1 Quiet Girl — $30 a month —
Catherine Street

Duration Leg-do. Sheer Looking As Nylon!
Big 4 ounce Bottle only 49 cents!
Creamy Golden Velvety Skin Tone!

I cross over and pass between the pillars of the Union Station. It's like walking between a giant's legs.

I'm imagining the Quiet Girl in the Bed Sitting Room spreading the Creamy Golden Velvety Skin guck on her legs to look like nylon stockings before she goes out to get the job Twice Weekly Evenings Ironing and Washing the Dishes. I know you wash dishes but I didn't know you ironed dishes.

Inside the station halfway down the long wide stairs I'm almost trampled by a crowd gone crazy. There's something big happening down there. People are stumbling down the stairs and sliding down the brass railings.

Everybody's yelling about money. Somebody giving money away. Somebody crazy. A crazy old guy throwing money around. A nutty millionaire is giving away fifty dollars! Fifty-dollar bills! Anybody in uniform. Hurry. He's down there! It's crazy! McLean from Merrickville! The millionaire nut from Merrickville is in town and he's gone berserk — he's giving anybody in uniform a fifty-dollar bill! My stars! Hurry!

The crowd is moving this way and that all of a sudden, like minnows all together, following the nut with the money.

The soldiers and sailors and airmen getting off the train can't believe it. Somebody's giving them $50. "Quick, over here! There's a nut giving out money!"

The minnows go this way and that way. Over here. There he goes! Now he's over there.

Then I see my father's third cousin once removed Doug Holmes. He's standing there in his red cap and his porter's uniform. He's not a soldier. But he's got a uniform.

The nut millionaire is going over to him. He's right up to him. My father's third cousin once removed stands at attention — he salutes. The millionaire gives him a fifty-dollar bill. Everybody is cheering! Doug Holmes is a hero! A hero in uniform!

I get down the stairs and wade into the crowd trying to find Doug Holmes and at least a big handful of money but I can't find him. He's gone. I'm too short to see.

Everybody is laughing and cheering and kissing the soldiers. There's a band playing and people are crying. The war's over and everything's going to be all right! In the band the cymbals are crashing and the drums pounding and the trombones are flashing in the light pouring in through the windows high up in the roof of the Union Station.

All of a sudden I'm standing right behind the millionaire. I stand stiff and straight.

He turns. He looks down at me. I salute. He's got a big roll of fifties in his fist. He peels one off. He puts it out. A hand comes over my head and grabs it. I look behind me. A sailor has the fifty. I look back.

The millionaire is gone.

Back outside in Confusion Square the crowd is big and wild now. The party is starting. The War Monument is covered with kids riding the huge black iron horses and sitting on the iron soldiers' shoulders and helmet heads and riding the big black gun. They're hiding under the wheels of the big black gun. They're under the wheels and under the horses' iron feet. If the horses move and the gun moves, the kids will be crushed. But they won't move. It's only a statue.

I'm thinking about a thing I heard a lady say in the Union Station. About her son. She said he was just a boy when he left but he's a man now he's back.

I'm thinking about Wash. Wash Tubbs. They were all saying he was too young when he went. Sixteen going on seventeen. But now he'll be seventeen going on eighteen. He was too young to fight they were saying. But now they'll say he's back and he's a man. Flight Lieutenant Terence Tubbs is a man now.

I'm wondering was he maybe in the station in the crowd and I didn't see him?

Wouldn't it be nice if he got a fifty-dollar bill? Wouldn't that be a good present when you come home? Have a crazy millionaire from Merrickville walk up and hand you fifty dollars. Welcome home, Wash! Here's fifty bucks! You're a man, now!

Things are happening all the way home.

People are talking about a big fight that happened at Bowle's Lunch on Rideau Street. Soldiers and sailors. Throwing food and soup at each other. Punching and kicking. Broke the big front window.

Slab wood trucks and coal trucks are driving around with the backs full of people with signs and flags. A milkman's horse still has his feed bag tied on his head. He's nodding to get the oats into his mouth. There's a flag stuck down into the bag. When the horse nods, the flag waves.

People are yelling at people on their verandahs.

"Soon there'll be no more gas rationing!"

"So what? You haven't got a car, anyway!"

A sign in the window of a store is a picture of the beautiful movie star Gale Storm. She uses Arid Cream Deodorant. So she won't smell bad. How could she ever smell bad, she's so beautiful?

"He was too young to be a pot washer at Imbro's Restaurant on Rideau but he wasn't too young to go to war!" That's what they said about Wash Tubbs.

"Forty-five million people killed! Imagine!"

"I can't imagine! I can't!"

Buckingham Throat Easy Cigarettes!

Two loaves of bread — 15 cents.

Household Finance — $25. Ten monthly payments of only $2.78 per month!

Delivery boys are driving other kids in their big iron grocery delivery baskets on the front of their bikes.

The bread man's horse has a weight tied to its ankle. The bread man is on somebody's front step — asleep. He smells like bread and his horse.

Big sign: Street Dance for Repats!

Yesterday's paper in the gutter. "Useless to Resist Any Longer!" the headline says.

They're singing Italian songs in front of Chicken Tetrazini's house. There's a piano out on the sidewalk. There's guys with big chests and sloping bellies dressed in black suits singing high and loud with one hand in the air.

In front of the fish store on the corner of St. Patrick and Cobourg the sign that said "HAN" on the hay wagon where they have the hanging noose now says:

"HANG HIROHITO!"

My father gets home just after me.

He's drunk but he's happy.

He has no money. He's going to go down to Household Finance and borrow $25.

My mother's upstairs in bed.

Everybody's yelling. The paper is out. It's in the store. It just arrived!

"Go down to the store and get the paper," my father says.

"Give me the money," I say.

"I have no money," he says. "Do you think I'm made of money? Do you think it grows on the bushes? Cash in a milk bottle. I see you brought home a wagonload of water this morning. No wonder I have no money. Ten cents for a little wagonload of free water! Cash a milk bottle and get us a paper, like a good lad!"

The paper is three cents. The refund on the milk bottle is two cents.

"I need the other cent," I say.

He empties his pockets. He pulls both pockets inside out. "See? Nothing. Go up and ask your mother." His pockets look like dead rats hanging.

I go upstairs. My mother's groaning on the bed. We find the cent and I head out. She had the cent in her good drawer. The drawer I'm not supposed to look in unless she's there. The one that smells like perfume where she keeps her best things. Secret silk handkerchiefs and lace and braid and brooches and barrettes and letters and a long hat pin with a carved head. The little square drawer slides in and out as quiet as satin. It's the best part of our house, this drawer. When I was a little kid I wanted to live in this drawer. Crawl inside it and stay there in the dark and never come out. With the perfume and the silk and the letters in the envelopes that smelled like roses.

The street is full.

They're kissing and dancing, bobby soxers and old men, flags are waving, car horns, noise makers, confetti, snakes of people, kids howling, dogs barking, babies and old people being pushed, boys running and darting, girls laughing and flirting and fixing each other's ribbons.

It starts pouring hot rain.

"It's only a shower! It's only a shower! Keep dancing. Let's get soaking wet!"

There's blocked traffic. Dynamite caps on the streetcar tracks.

Decorated cars and ice trucks and milk wagons, beer in the gutter, church bells, firecrackers, rockets, whistles, bonfires, sticks banging pots, little parades, banging washboards, blowing old bugles, burning and hanging Emperor Hirohito, stringing paper on the wires, soaked to the skin, sirens, streetcar bells, train whistles, school bells, laughing and crying, kissing and hugging, shouting and climbing, canons and air raid sirens, loud radios and record players turned up full, throwing everything up in the air, riding on the roofs of cars and streetcars, drums and baseball bats and tin pans, homemade costumes, men on crutches, kids in bathing suits in the rain, butter pails to pound, "Open post office — a penny a kiss," "Hail, hail, the Gang's All Here!" they're singing. An old woman is crying against a post. "The navy can kiss more girls than the army!" Smoke bombs, toilet paper, firemen, and police, and the crowds sing "Roll Out the Barrel!"

I'm running with my milk bottle, leaping the puddles and dodging the people. I'm dodging machine gun bullets like Alan Ladd does in the movies.

Some people are rocking a streetcar, trying to tip it over. "Heave! Heave! Heave!" the crowd is yelling and clapping.

There are three cement steps up into the store on the corner. I can make all three in one leap. I've done it many times. It's easy. I'm a good jumper. In mid-air I glance up to see if Claudette who wears no underpants is on her balcony.

I fall into the steps and the milk bottle breaks. My leg is sliced and so is my arm. Lots of blood. Nobody pays any attention. Nobody sees.

Now I can't get the paper. My father will be mad. This morning a wagon of water. Now blood instead of the paper.

I go into the store anyway. It's crowded. The owner doesn't care. He's giving away free gum and candy and bottles of Orange Crush. Everybody's grabbing.

I take a paper and run out. Without paying. Nobody yells, "Stop, thief!" like they do in the Alan Ladd movies.

"ALLIES ISSUE 'CEASE FIRE.' JAPS QUIT!" the headline on the paper says.

There's blood on it as I read it.

In front of Mrs. Tubbs's house is a crowd acting different. They're not singing and dancing. They are watching some people hugging Mrs. Tubbs on her front porch.

I go up to the back of the crowd.

There's a stack of hot horseballs steaming in rainwater. The horseballs remind me of Wash Tubbs playing hockey. Wash is the best stickhandler on the street. In the winter we use a frozen horseball as a puck. We use the street as our rink. We use the snowbanks as the boards of the rink. Our rink is five blocks long. Our rink is Cobourg Street from Rideau Street down to St. Patrick Street. Everybody on the street plays.

Wash can stickhandle a frozen horseball through everybody all the way down the street.

There's usually two teams.

Everybody's on one team.

Wash Tubbs is on the other team. It's Wash Tubbs against everybody. He starts at the top of the street and stickhandles the frozen horseball all the way down to the bottom of the street, five blocks, through every kid that wants to try and stop him.

He's also the best shooter on the street.

He can wrist shot a frozen horseball and knock the mailman's hat off.

He can put one up on Claudette's balcony.

He can drive one through your mail slot.

He's the best.

I push into the crowd. Closer to the front. Closer to the steps of the verandah where Mrs. Tubbs is.

I hear. I hear them say. I hear something unbelievable.

Wash is dead. Wash Tubbs is killed. In the jungle in Burma. I don't believe it.

His mother got the letter a few minutes ago. The mailman said he was sorry.

Mrs. Tubbs is howling. Nobody knows what to do.

One of the dynamite caps on the streetcar tracks blows up and everybody cheers. It's lots of fun.

"Just one more day," Mrs. Tubbs is saying with her tears. "Just one more day, for the love of God!"

The paper is so filthy with blood and rain and mud that you can hardly read it. I walk slowly home.

I hand the paper to my father but he doesn't even look at it. He throws it. I'm trying to tell my father about Wash. He won't listen.

Another dynamite cap goes off.

My father's stuttering and spitting drunk.

"Run!" he says. "Run as fast as you can! Baby's comin'. Go up, run, and get Dr. Church! Run."

I head up Cobourg Street to Rideau, through the cheering crowds. I'm crying.

Alan Ladd never cries.

Running like mad for the doctor through the screaming and the explosions and the smoke.

And I'm covered with blood.

I'm thinking about my little brother who is almost here in the world.

What he'll be like.

What I'll be like.

Summer 1943: Brian Doyle fishing behind the ice house on the Ottawa River with the ice house cat.

BRIAN DOYLE *grew up to become a high school English teacher and a superb writer of fiction, the first Canadian to have been shortlisted (1998) for the prestigious international Hans Christian Andersen Award, and the winner of many Canadian literary awards, some of them three times. Brian interpreted his assignment for* Too Young to Fight *in his usual creative way. He has not been asked to vouch for the literal truth of every element in his chapter. This editor suspects that Brian has brought certain elements in his life together, "tweaking" them here and there for dramatic effect. Elsewhere he tells how his father's storytelling abilities inspired him. However, the films described, the ads, and Brian's part of wartime Ottawa are all authentic. Brian's child self was surely a version of the narrator, and I do not for a moment doubt that his fishing buddy in the photograph was, as stated, the ice house cat.*

INDEX